For Ad, Isaac and Noah,
and Enid the cat,
love always.

MAD ABOUT THE HOUSE

How to decorate your home with style

KATE WATSON-SMYTH

PAVILION

First published in the United Kingdom in 2018 by
Pavilion
43 Great Ormond Street
London
WC1N 3HZ

ISBN 978-1-91159-542-7

A CIP catalogue record for this book is available from the British Library.

10 9 8 7 6

Reproduction by Mission Productions, Hong Kong
Printed and bound by 1010 Printing International Ltd, China

www.pavilionbooks.com

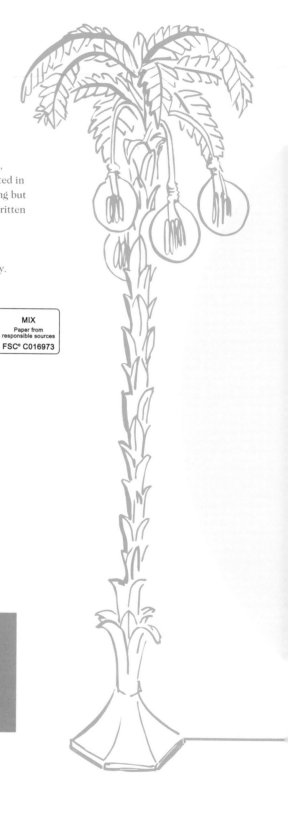

CONTENTS

YOUR HOME, YOUR STORY

having enough storage; for the lack of space to hang the towels after a shower; or the fact that you can only open the dishwasher when the bin is closed. It's like a bad marriage that you can't escape.

It doesn't need to be like that. We have the amount of space that the builder and the bank manager (or landlord) saw fit to give us, and we need to make this relationship work. Yes, there has to be some compromise, but there should also be a whole lot of love, a few laughs and plenty of moments that make your heart sing. Like the one when you realise that, for all the crumpled shirts in the overstuffed wardrobe and the mug stains on the coffee table, there is really, truly, nowhere else you would rather be. That you are home. That you are, despite its idiosyncrasies and multiple annoying habits, mad about your house.

This book will help you define your personal style, teach you about the perils of Pinterest and help you work out what colours you like. It will lead you around your home room by room, looking at all the elements you need to consider in order to make the best of what you've got. The answer isn't always ripping down the walls; instead, it's often about using the space to its best advantage.

We'll look at the lighting, the flooring, the storage and the layout. We'll discuss the key pieces of furniture, from how to buy a sofa to choosing a mattress; the pros and cons of different kitchen worktops; and how to give your room that key element that makes it uniquely yours.

Every room should have something that draws you in. An amazing piece of furniture, a funky light, a family heirloom. So come with me around your own home, whether it's a one-bedroom flat or a ten-bedroom villa – they all have elements in common – and let's see how we can make it tell your story.

What finally matters is that your house works the way you want it to. And that it is a pleasant place to be in.

Ray Eames, 1959

FIND YOUR STYLE

I'm going to make a radical assumption here: that you've been making your own sartorial choices for some time, and that it's been a while since your mum stopped choosing your clothes. If you haven't, you should probably pass this book along to the person who is making those decisions for you.

If you're still reading, we can assume that you have a pretty good idea of what you like to wear. But many of you will be paralysed with indecision when it comes to dressing your house – and you do need to think of it in those terms. In many ways it's easier to find clothes for your house because your house doesn't have fat days, or hangover days, or days when it can't quite be bothered and just wants to wear tracksuit bottoms and lie on the sofa with a packet of biscuits. Your house, flat, penthouse, apartment or cottage is the same size all year round and probably the only thing that changes is the light, which depends on the weather outside and the time of day (we'll come to that later on).

In the meantime, the first thing you need to bear in mind when you're planning your décor, whether it's a full refurb or a gentle tweak, is that you *do* know what you like, it's just that you haven't quite worked out how to relate your favourite shoes to the wardrobe you want to put them in.

Which leads me neatly to the wardrobe, for that is where you must start. Go to it now. Open the doors, or the drawers. Stand in front of the rail and see what colours are there. And yes, I appreciate that you have nothing to wear to that party at the weekend,

but that's a different book. We're simply looking at the colours for now, because that is the first clue to finding your style. If you are comfortable wearing it, you will be comfortable living in it. It's that simple.

My wardrobe, for example, has no blue in it. And, it turns out, there is no blue in my house. At least, there wasn't until a couple of years ago when I randomly bought a navy blue silk shirt. Then suddenly, when ordering a sofa bed for the loft conversion, I decided that it had to be navy blue, a colour I haven't worn since school, and which had never appeared anywhere in my decisions before. My wardrobe is basically black, grey, ivory and various shades of pink. Guess what? So is my house.

Now, I'm sure there will be many of you who say you only wear black suits or sensible dark clothes to work. But what about the weekend? What colours are your socks? Your earrings, your ties – does anyone still wear those? – or the cover on your smartphone? And if it's still black, all black, then congratulations: you are massively on-trend and quite possibly Danish. Or you're an architect, and will know exactly how you want your home to look, regardless of anything I might have to say.

When you have worked out a palette of the colours that make you comfortable, you need to think about the proportions you will use them in. Once again, your clothes can help with this. It's like getting dressed. You might wear black all over with a red bag, zebra-print earrings or contrasting laces in your shoes. You might prefer to colour block: a pale blue shirt with orange trousers, ivory trainers and a matching bag (that was Victoria Beckham a few months ago). But you can see already how you're mixing up the colours to create outfits without panicking. Even if you go into a shop and buy everything off the mannequin head to toe, that's fine if you like it all. That outfit has been put together by experts, so you can be confident that the colours and proportions are good.

It's exactly the same with a room. Pick a colour – perhaps a neutral, let's keep it simple to start with – and put that on the largest area: your walls. That's your clothes, or the main thing you are choosing to wear that day – a dress or trousers, for example. Choose a second colour for the largest piece of furniture, say the sofa. This is your top or jacket. Add some pattern in the form of cushions: your earrings or necklace. The accessories – rugs, armchairs – are the final colour: your shoes and bag.

The idea is basically 60 per cent one colour, 30 per cent another and 10 per cent for the finishing touches. So if it's black jeans, black-and-white striped shirt, red boots and gold earrings, you could reinterpret it as grey walls and a grey sofa, pink cushions and brass lamps. You see, you don't even need to do maths for this formula – just think of it as getting dressed. If you like to add a patterned scarf as a final flourish to your outfit, then that's a sofa throw.

Once you're confident with this method you can afford to play around, substituting mismatching earrings or a funky handbag for an unusual table lamp with bird legs or a mirror with a huge frame. After all, haven't we all got that slightly random thing in our wardrobe that we probably shouldn't have bought but which makes us happy when we wear it? Mine is a vintage Miu Miu bag covered in silver sequins that practically made my mother cry when I took it to a country pub for lunch on a Tuesday afternoon. I'm not sure if it was the bag, the location or the timing that did it, but it made me so happy I didn't care.

The equivalent in my house is a 6ft brass lamp in the shape of a palm tree. I still don't know how I got it past my husband, but I love it every single day and it looks perfect with the dark grey walls and splashes of pink that accessorise my sitting room. That's the wow factor in that room, the element that pulls everything together and gives the space its personality. Without that lamp it's a tasteful, well put-together room. With the lamp it's fun and witty and cool. I realise it might be a little over the top for some of you, but this book is about helping you find your own palm trees.

When you get dressed, do you have a signature item? Are you known for your flamboyant earrings, your tiny tattoo or your cool socks? Perhaps you have an amazing handbag, cool glasses or always wear a black T-shirt whatever the weather. You need to find that signature element that is always in your outfit and make sure that your home has it too.

Having dealt with the colours and proportions of your outfit and your room, you now need to think about your style. Yep, it's back to the wardrobe again. Do you wear structured suits for work and perhaps keep to the same simple shapes at the weekend? Have you considered the clean, minimal lines of mid-century modern furniture? If your wardrobe tends towards the monochrome with the odd splash of colour (not pattern), think about the muted greys and architectural lines

of Scandinavian style. Do you have a bit of a rebellious streak when it comes to clothes – a ripped jean, a statement sleeve or a pair of metallic boots? Perhaps the industrial look is more your thing, with its exposed brickwork and leather sofas, reclaimed floorboards and metal task lamps. Or are you a full-on glamour girl with lots of gold accessories and patterns, in which case a bit of boho might be right: mismatched chairs, tassels on the cushions and metallic motifs. If you live in jeans and spend money on interesting tops and T-shirts, modern rustic could be the way forward: natural textures like wood, concrete and stone with luxury elements thrown in such as brass, marble and velvet. It's all there staring you in the face. You just need to look for it.

But there is one caveat: just as you should never buy that garment thinking you will slim down into it – you won't – so you should never decorate your home for the person you think you want to be. Instead, decorate for a slightly better version of who you are. If you like cooking and want to improve, buy a great, professional range oven. If you prepare meals simply in order to stave off collapse, choose a functioning cooker and buy some great bar stools instead.

THE PERILS OF
PINTEREST

Beware the Pinterest Board, my love
The pins that tempt, the pictures that stun
Beware the images that lure, and shun
The ones that call you just for fun

(with apologies to Lewis Carroll)

Pinterest is your frenemy. There, I've said it. It might fool you into thinking it's helping you by being the best interior designer friend you never had, but just when you've come to rely on it for inspiration, it will betray you by showing you new pictures that are at odds with your instincts, and whisper seductively that you should change your plans.

It will build up your confidence only to shatter it just when you thought you'd created the perfect scheme, and it will leave you confused and nervous and wondering if you've done the right thing. There you are on a Saturday morning with a coffee, sitting in that little patch of sun, laptop open. You're in visual heaven as you pin all the gorgeous images of sofas, rooms, walls. The odd pair of shoes sneaks in, a few recipe ideas and ooh look, a holiday destination! Four hours later, you've lost all sight of the scheme you thought you wanted. Sound familiar? I've lost count of the number of clients who have rung me up to say they have 647 pins on their kitchen board, but now have no idea if they should even be doing the kitchen before the sitting room, much less what colour and style they think they want.

If you're going to have a successful relationship with Pinterest you need to show it who's boss right from the start. Don't let it be that girl in the changing room who persuades you to buy the dress in the wrong shape, size or colour when you instinctively know you're making a mistake. I'm going to show you how to avoid falling into that trap when it comes to finding your home style inspiration. I can't promise it will get rid of the girl in the changing room, but it might give you the confidence to listen to your instincts and ignore her.

Pinterest is a labyrinth, and you need to leave a trail of breadcrumbs to mark your path to the exit. One client told me in no uncertain terms that she didn't care what I suggested for her house as long as there was no blue, because the only thing she knew for certain was that she didn't like blue. I didn't have to look at more than about six images before it became clear that she loved blue – navy blue, at least: it was in every picture and on every board. She just couldn't see it any more because the whole thing was a riot of colours and styles, ideas and inspiration, most of which were completely unsuitable for her Edwardian terrace in north London.

Before we get onto how to manage Pinterest, let me just throw in a word about followers. Pinterest is not social media, it's a search engine. Unless you are running a business that needs traffic, you don't need followers. This is relevant because there's always the temptation to add a pin that will get lots of repins. It may be Pinterest clickbait, but it won't help you design your living room. For our purposes it's probably better to keep your boards secret, at least to start with. That way it's easier to be honest with yourself about what you're pinning because nobody is looking or judging you. Forget about the girl in the changing room.

So here's how to do it. First, get it out of your system: create three boards, give each one a name (let's say A, B and C) and go. Run along the corridors of images, grabbing pictures you like from every room and sticking them on board A. Pin fast and loose and go with your gut. Run until that initial joyful sprint has slowed to a jog and from there to a steady walk. When you get that feeling that you've eaten an entire box of chocolates and just need to lie down for a while, stop. Close the computer and go and do something completely different.

When you return, go back to board A but don't add any more pins. Just let your eyes float over what you have in front of you. Scroll up and down – you don't need to look at them in detail yet. With your fresh, rested eyes you will immediately notice that there is a uniformity of colour or a palette of two or three shades that keep reappearing. There will also be some that jump out because they jar. Make a note of the dominant shades: they will be the basis of your new scheme. It might be the walls, it might be a piece of furniture, but either way, you've just found your starting point. Don't worry about how you're going to use it for now, we're just window shopping at this stage.

Now it's time to work on boards B and C. You need to go through all those images on board A and, for each one, ask yourself if you pinned it because it was well styled and you just liked looking at it, or if it contained something that could actually work in your house. I am constantly drawn to blush pink rooms that are filled with plants. I spent a weekend putting blush pink paint samples on the bedroom wall, and persuaded my husband that it was the right colour for us. But the reality was that I didn't like any of them enough to live with. I had been so persuasive in my desire for this shade that in the end I had to talk him back out of it. And you know something else? I have eight tops in various shades of blush pink: long sleeve, short sleeve,

knitted and silk. I don't wear any of them. They look gorgeous folded up on the shelf against the (eventual) mid-grey of my bedroom walls, but that is where they stay, pretty and folded. I should have taken my own advice and looked at my clothes before I bought the tester pots.

Be honest with yourself. Could something like that work in your house, or is it just lovely to look at? It's no good pinning endless pictures of industrial warehouse conversions if you live in a modern semi or a small mansion flat. If you really do like it, but it won't work in your house, move it to board B. This is for the fantasy houses,

the rooms of your dreams. So now you have two boards: one for everything that's caught your eye, and one for your fantasy house – the wraparound veranda with swing seat, as opposed to your balcony overlooking the bins from the Chinese restaurant below. The homes that a lottery win and a job in another country might bring you. But for better or worse, the house that the builder and the mortgage broker let you have is the one we are dealing with here. So move anything that will actually work in your real house to board C – it's where we pin the practical looks and ideas that will inspire and guide your interior renovation.

Once you've begun to separate fantasy from reality, you're making progress. You are moving some pins from your first board to the fantasy board (B) and some to the reality board (C). Most importantly, you are beginning to build a collection of things on board C that could potentially work in your home – a sofa style, a bookshelf arrangement, a gallery wall – but you need to refine it still further.

Go through the images and ask yourself why you pinned them. Was it the colour of the walls? Was it the furniture? That particular chair or the lamp next to it? Start sifting through your pictures, work out the appeal of each one and label it very simply: chair, light, rug. It's about the individual objects rather than the whole room; you won't be able to copy the whole room exactly, and it has probably been styled and decluttered for the photograph, so it doesn't represent real life.

Once again, if you're being honest with yourself, you'll start to see a pattern emerge. Your fantasy board (B) is going to be looking pretty darn sexy by this point, and no doubt contains polished plaster walls, vintage chandeliers and Crittall windows overlooking the designer velvet sofa you saw in a magazine last week,

but that's where you go when you're dreaming of jacking it all in and jetting off to live in Mexico on your lottery winnings.

Back to the reality board (C). Keep going through the images and asking yourself: why do I want this? Where will I put it? Will it go with the rest of my house? If you do this part properly – and it's worth taking a little time over it – you'll end up with a board that's both realistic and inspirational.

We'll deal with each room individually later in the book but, in brief, you should by now have pinned a few sofas that will work for your actual family, the family that lies around on a Saturday afternoon watching films and creasing the cushions. Not the fantasy family which sits with perfect posture, makes polite conversation and plays board games. And you should have chosen a colour that you like to wear so that you know you'll be comfortable living in it.

And you can plan a trip to the shops with confidence because now, at last, you are in charge of Pinterest and you know how to make it work for you. You've started to gain a sense of how your space should look and feel to reflect the real you.

HOW TO USE PINTEREST: A CHECKLIST

☐ Pin everything that takes your fancy to board A.

☐ Walk away and do something completely different for a while.

☐ Scroll up and down board A, observing common elements of colour and style.

☐ Delete the pins that are obviously jarring.

☐ Go through the remaining pins and ask yourself what you liked about them. Be honest.

☐ If you like them but they won't work in your current house or room, stick them on board B for daydreaming/inspirational purposes.

☐ Go through the pins that are left on board A. Ask yourself what you like about each one – the rug, the light, the chair.

☐ Label accordingly and move them to board C – the reality board..

☐ Repeat with each pin until board C is full of achievable ideas. You will get faster as you get used to this editing process.

☐ Board C is your room (or home) scheme. You can refine it and add to it, but try to keep to a maximum of 50 pins or it will be too big to be useful. You don't need six pictures of navy blue kitchen cabinets. One will do; it's just a visual reminder.

A WORD ABOUT COLOUR

We respond to colour in three ways – psychologically, personally and culturally – and there is very little we can do to change those instinctive reactions. Many of us shun the colours we wore when we were a kid for the rest of our lives. Others return to the same colour again and again because, without understanding why, it makes us feel happy or relaxed. Then there are the cultural associations, such as that pink is for girls, red stimulates the appetite and white is the most calming shade of all.

Choosing which colour to put on the walls is often the hardest part of your design scheme to decide on, yet it's the easiest to change. Be bold. Why not? You can always paint over it. As we saw earlier, the first place to start when choosing a colour is your wardrobe, because if you're comfortable wearing it you'll be comfortable living in it. The next thing to consider is why you are painting the woodwork and the ceilings white. Seriously, stop for a minute and think. Is there a valid reason or did the builder just assume that was what you wanted? Is that what the house you grew up in was like?

To return to the wardrobe: if you wear an ankle strap on your shoe, doesn't your leg look shorter? Exactly. So paint the skirting boards the same colour as the walls to create the impression of a higher ceiling, and the architrave around the door and, while we're at it, the back of the door. We're not usually trapped in a room, needing to be able to spot the door easily at all times; it can afford to blend in. It will make the room look bigger, not to mention being more relaxing because the eye won't be distracted by the wall colour being broken up by the architectural features.

As for the colour itself, you don't have to adhere slavishly to colour psychology, but it's fun to know a little about the subject. Take those three statements from the first paragraph: pink for girls, red for appetite and white for calm. Well, pink was actually for boys until the 1940s, when it was changed by US clothing manufacturers as part of a marketing scheme. Red is the colour of luck and money; it is orange that is said to stimulate the appetite. White is the colour of mourning in China.

In this chapter we'll take a stroll around the rainbow, take a look at the key qualities of various colours and consider which room they are ideally suited to. Every colour has both positive and negative attributes and a little knowledge might give you some food for thought. You can paint your kitchen yellow to stimulate conversation, but you might not want it in the bedroom. Discover which colours work best in which rooms – and ignore your findings if you dare.

RED

Red is perhaps the most manipulative shade on the colour wheel. It's associated with extremes of emotion, both good and bad: passion and anger, fortune and fury, blood and money, warnings and celebrations. We roll out the red carpet on a red letter day, and if that goes well we might paint the town red afterwards. Or perhaps we're down to our last red cent after buying an outfit for the party, although the invitation might have been nothing more than a red herring anyway.

Red is the first colour of the rainbow and the one we always see, even when the others are nothing more than a vague, shimmering presence, visible only because we know they are there. When it comes to our homes, despite red being the colour of passion, it should rarely be used in a bedroom, probably because it raises energy levels too much and therefore isn't conducive to a good night's sleep. There's a fine line between a night of passion and a blazing row; just ask Christian Grey.

Red works better downstairs as it stimulates conversation, which is why you so often find it in the dining room. According to Chinese philosophy, red is the colour of luck, which is why so many of their restaurants are painted that colour. You enter, think your appetite is being stimulated, eat loads, pay a huge bill and it's the owner who gets lucky.

It's not surprising, given all these associations, that red creates a strong first impression. Use it in your hallway if you dare. But before you paint the sitting room, bear in mind that there's a reason why red is so prevalent in Formula One, and it's because when we see red our reactions speed up and become more forceful. However, that boost of energy may be short-lived and, crucially, red can reduce your ability to think analytically. The key to using red in interiors, then, is to keep it to an accent colour. A muted red in

a monochrome scheme will provide a cheering splash of colour or, paired with dark blue, will create a more rustic palette.

Before we leave red, what about its gentler cousin, pink? As we've seen, it wasn't always for girls. In June 1918 an article in *Earnshaw's Infants' Department* (a trade magazine for children's fashion) said: 'The generally accepted rule is pink for the boys, and blue for the girls. The reason is that pink, being a more decided and stronger colour, is more suitable for the boy, while blue, which is more delicate and dainty, is prettier for the girl.' Pink is also a calming colour. In 2013, it was reported that after a Swiss prison painted around 30 cells pink, anger levels were reduced within 15 minutes. On that tranquil note, we will leave red and move round the colour wheel to orange.

ORANGE If red is the toddler of the colour wheel – all extremes of emotion and mercurial temperament – then orange is your new BFF. The colour of companionship and laughter, appetite and intelligence, orange is the feel-good shade: happy, social and extrovert. Be careful, though, as it can also appear frivolous and give the impression that things are not being taken too seriously. Use it sparingly at work or in places where you need to impress.

In addition to its fun and optimistic side, orange is also said to be associated with good value, which suddenly puts the EasyJet logo in a new light, doesn't it? Think also of Homebase and Sainsbury's in the UK and Home Depot in the US. That's all the more reason to be wary of using too much of it in a meeting room or hotel, as, while you clearly want to give the impression that your product is good value, it is firmly associated with the budget end of the market. (Although that doesn't explain why luxury French brand Hermès uses it. Does it want to persuade us that it's more affordable than its prices would have us believe?)

Mind you, it doesn't matter what the psychologists tell us, because it's often instinctive and cultural reactions that come first. For Americans, the colour orange may make them think of prison or chain gangs. For the Dutch, it's the Royal Family and the national football team. But for Hindus, orange (or saffron) is a sacred and auspicious shade, whereas in Northern Ireland it is strongly associated with the Protestants, giving it both a religious and political significance. While we can do little about our instinctive reactions to a colour, orange is said to decrease feelings of irritation (unless you're an American criminal, a Dutch republican or an Irish Catholic), which makes it a good colour to use in busy rooms or spaces where lots of people congregate, as it will encourage them to be well-behaved and cheerful. If you work from home, a splash of orange can give you a much healthier energy boost than a chocolate biscuit at four o'clock every afternoon.

Having said that, it is orange, not red, that is the colour of appetite, so be careful if you paint your kitchen in this shade or you may end up piling on the pounds. Likewise, if you have too much of it in your office you may spend more time snacking than working. As an accent in a dining room it can work well since, used in moderation, it is said to aid digestion and encourage socialising.

Something else to bear in mind is that orange hasn't really been used in interiors since the 1970s, and seems inextricably linked to that decade. Back then, the lightbulbs were tungsten and gave off a lovely, warm glow. The soft reds, browns and oranges that were characteristic of that period reacted well to this incandescent light and made our homes look cosy and warm. However, with the move to LEDs and low-energy bulbs with the cool blue light, those colours reacted badly and fell out of favour. This is the real reason why we all love grey now – it works well under the cool blue light that we live in.

Pair your orange with black or charcoal for a less aggressive take on the red-and-black combination. It's great with every shade of blue, too, from navy to aqua for a rustic kitchen or cheery bathroom. But if it feels a little too vibrant for a room

in which you want to relax, you can tone it down to a soft peach or choose a darker burnt orange shade so that it doesn't overpower. If you want it in the bedroom, keep it to the accents or choose a paler shade, otherwise you might be too stimulated to sleep.

Orange will also make a room seem warmer than it is, so use it in the sitting room and turn the heating down a notch. This brings us neatly back to the value-for-money aspect of this most vibrant of colours.

The feel-good shade of the colour wheel, orange
is happy and extravert, warm and optimistic.
If it's too bright, tone it down to a soft peach
or darken it to burnt orange which will pair
beautifully with grey – dark or light – as well as
shades of blue from navy to teal.

YELLOW

If orange is the feel-good shade of the colour wheel – all laughter and friendship, appetite and intelligence – then where does yellow take us? When mixed with red it creates that friendly orange but, on its own, yellow can provoke a range of quite extreme reactions.

Think first of the buttery yellow kitchen that seems permanently filled with sunshine and loving families who never argue in the morning. But harden that shade to one that is brighter and deeper and it takes on a more aggressive tone. Yellow and black are used on danger signs almost as often as red and signifies hazard or, in the US, a crime scene. Used in this combination, yellow can provoke feelings of anxiety and agitation. Don't forget, too, that yellow is said to be the colour of cowardice: the yellow belly.

Like the other colours, yellow also has different meanings in different countries. In the UK and the US, it is used to symbolise remembrance and hope (remember the song? *Tie a yellow ribbon round the old oak tree)* and is often the colour of liberalism. In Japan it represents courage, while in China it was the colour of the emperors who often dressed in it, possibly because it is the closest to gold. In India it is the colour of merchants.

Aside from its negative and cultural connotations, what about the positive? We talk about someone having a sunny disposition, which is clearly a reference to yellow. It is also said to be the colour of knowledge, connecting with the left, or logical, side of the brain to stimulate new ideas and work out mental challenges.

When it comes to using yellow in your home or hotel, it's great for hallways and entrance spaces as well as for breakfast rooms and kitchens, where its sunny properties will welcome people into the room. If you have too much yellow, you can tone it down with purple, its complimentary colour on the colour wheel, and if that seems a bit too much, try a purple-based grey for a classic combination. Or use the colours next to it on the colour wheel for a more harmonious palette, in this case varieties of orange and red or green.

Don't forget that this doesn't have to mean pillar-box red or bright grass green; there are endless versions and more subtle shades.

Unluckily for yellow, it seems to be one of the most polarising colours of the rainbow. Those who like it seem to love it, while those who dislike it really hate it.

However, a small burst of yellow is unlikely to create too many problems, especially if it's a bowl of lemons or a large bunch of daffodils on the kitchen table.

GREEN

Ah, green, the colour of nature, restfulness and calm, of serenity and peace, rejuvenation and harmony...

But wait a minute. How many times have you met people who say they won't have a green car? Whose front door can be any colour as long as it's not green? Who feel certain that green is the harbinger of bad luck? And what about the green-eyed monster? Or that time you felt a bit green about the gills? On the other hand, we are given the green light on a project or might have green fingers when it comes to the garden.

Once again in our tour of the rainbow, we find that for every positive association of a colour there is a negative to cancel it out. Karen Haller, a business colour and branding expert, tells of a friend who, following a tough divorce, decided to paint her entire flat green. It was to be a restful haven that would bring peace and harmony back into her life. But over time stagnant ponds turn green, warns Haller. The friend began to feel drained and tired. Her home was no longer the energising place she had imagined. She had left the green on the walls for too long and over time its negative emotional qualities began to surface. In order to move on, she needed to redecorate, from which we can take the good news

that there's always an excuse to change a colour scheme.

Do be warned, though: green is one shade that can really change under artificial light, so you need to check it in both daylight and electric light before you commit, otherwise what looks fresh and energising in the day might turn blue and cold at night.

The key to getting it right is what you put with it. Sage, mint and forest green are perfect with shades of pink. If it works in nature, then it works indoors too. Emerald green is brilliant in a monochromatic scheme – use black and white as the basis for this, or soften it to charcoal and ivory. All greens work with the metals silver, brass and copper. Of course, one of the best ways to bring green inside is with plants. Bring living greenery into your home to encourage feelings of positivity and growth. But don't forget to mist them regularly to keep the leaves clean and shiny; it's pretty obvious that dry and decaying plants will not have the intended effect.

Speaking of effects, there was a study recently which found that one particular shade of green was the ugliest colour in the world. Opaque Couche, or Pantone 448C, is a sort of dirty olive and, said the survey, so hideous that governments in the UK,

France and Ireland were thinking of using it on cigarette packets to put people off smoking. It has been used for this purpose in Australia since 2012. It's not a bad colour, but it's a long way from the fresh shades of emerald that will bring positivity into your office.

Another survey, by Dulux, in 2011 found that while blue was the most popular colour in the world, it was closely followed by green. The company found that 23 per cent of people over 50 said green was their favourite, but that dropped to 14 per cent of those under 50. More recently, YouGov carried out a worldwide survey of 10 countries across four continents and while blue won all over the world, green came second in the US, China and Thailand.

Let's not forget also that green is the colour of money, and who wouldn't want to encourage some more of that to come their way? Money, growth and success are all linked to it. Now, which wall do you want to paint first?

Green is the colour of the moment, whether it's plants – real or faux – or paint. A touch of greenery will enhance any room as it really does bring a little of the outdoors in. Emerald green is magical with black and white, but any of the forest greens are both restful and calming. If you are using it on the walls make sure you check that you like it in both natural and electric light, as it can change dramatically between the two – what looks fresh and energising by day can look cold and blue by night.

BLUE

As we've seen, blue is the world's favourite colour. Time after time in surveys this restful shade comes out on top. In 2017, Dulux, which sells paint in 80 countries around the globe, chose a soft, greyish blue as its colour of the year. This decision was based on an international panel of experts who look at social trends, economic forecasts, fashion and food to see what direction the world is heading in. The answer was Denim Drift – a colour of our everyday, said the company. It's the sky above, the clothes we wear and it unites all the other colours. Pantone also announced a strong cobalt blue as one of its colours of 2017. It doesn't matter which variation of this shade you prefer, there's going to be a lot of it about for some time to come.

The Victorians thought that blue kept flies away, so their kitchens were often painted blue for hygiene reasons in the pre-refrigeration era. Other research (since slightly debunked but worth a go if you're desperate) found that serving food on a blue plate makes you eat less. Blue has also become the colour of communication. Colour theory says that's yellow, but if you look at the logos of both Facebook and Twitter, it would seem that blue and white has taken over – in the online world, at least.

In its darker form, navy, blue has long been a fashion favourite and there is barely a house in the Hamptons which hasn't made a nautical reference in its décor somewhere with a soft blue-and-white palette.

But what about the feelings blue evokes? As with all the colours on the wheel, there is both positivity and negativity. This is a colour universally associated with conservatism and a sense of old-fashioned common sense and reliability. Looked at from the other side, blue also conveys a sense of authority and trust. It is not a colour that likes to be rushed, but to reflect and analyse. There is nothing spontaneous about blue.

Blue is also a shorthand for feeling slightly down in the dumps. In *Breakfast at Tiffany's*, Holly Golightly refers to feeling blue 'because you're getting fat and maybe it's been raining too long, you're just sad, that's all'. On the other hand, blue is a deeply calming colour. Think of lying on your back staring up at the sky and letting your worries drift away, or sitting on a beach and watching the waves wash away your problems.

When it comes to interiors, blue tends to make decorators nervous as it is a colour that can appear cold. While there are many shades in the cool end of the spectrum – and should help to avoid heated arguments and to lower blood pressure – it can also be a strong, warm colour. Navy blue has been gathering momentum in interiors recently as the fashion for dark neutrals is growing. Dark colours on your walls make everything else stand out.

Pale shades of blue, with their calming attributes, work well in bedrooms. A stronger blue, as the colour of social media, might encourage a spot of breakfast chat in the kitchen, which could come in handy if you have teenagers glued to screens.

As for what to pair it with, yellow is its opposite on the colour wheel, so that will always work. Move round the wheel slightly and you arrive at dark blue with orange – think of the spicy colours of North Africa. A watery blue with natural floorboards will evoke the idea of sand and sea, and a more relaxing combination would be hard to find. And while the old adage 'blue and green should never be seen' might hold true for many, there are plenty of shades of each that do work in harmony. In other words, using blue doesn't need to make you feel blue.

INDIGO

It might sound obvious, but the next colour in the rainbow, indigo, is a combination of what came before and what will follow: blue and violet. And therein lies the problem. Is it actually a deep, dark navy or is it an intense, inky purple?

And that's not the end of it. In some modern depictions of the rainbow, indigo isn't even there at all. Take a close look at the Gay Pride rainbow. There are only six colours visible; indigo has vanished. It's the same on the Pink Floyd album Dark Side of the Moon. So what happened to indigo? Well, apparently Sir Isaac Newton, who first named the colours of the rainbow, actually only saw five. But he believed in the power of seven as the number of mystical perfection, so he added orange and indigo.

Whether you think it has a place in the rainbow or not, the psychological properties of indigo don't change. It is the colour of magic and ritual, intuition and perception, integrity and sincerity. On the negative side, it can be narrow-minded and intolerant, prone to fanaticism and addiction. This colour draws in both the alcoholic and the workaholic.

'Indigo children' are said to possess special, sometimes supernatural, traits according to a concept developed in the 1970s by Nancy Ann Tappe, who studied the links between personality and colour. According to her website, allaboutindigos.com, famous indigo people include Barack Obama, Chelsea Clinton, Mark Zuckerberg and Eminem.

Indigo has been an important colour in several cultures for thousands of years. It comes from the plant *Indigofera tinctoria,* which is native to the tropics. Compatible with all natural fibres, it was once the only source of blue dye but could also be combined with other natural dyes to create different colours.

While there are many stories about the invention of blue jeans, there are few about why the denim was dyed this colour in the first place. One theory is that indigo was the best-known natural dye until the end of the nineteenth century, and thus became linked with workwear. In addition to this, indigo's ability to bind itself steadfastly to fabric and its dark colour made it a practical choice at a time when washing clothes was hard work.

But psychological properties and historical anecdotes aside, what about putting it on your walls? When it comes to interiors, indigo will certainly make an impact, but you need to consider it carefully in a room where you will be spending long periods of time, as it can overwhelm. However, it is perfect for that rich gentleman's club look or to create a feeling of luxury in a bathroom. And, while blue is the colour of communication, indigo is more about the inner self, so it won't be encouraging lively conversation.

Inky blue is increasingly fashionable in interiors at the moment and, when paired with brass – which has also made a comeback in recent years – it creates a sense of opulence and luxury. If you don't want it on your walls, think about bringing it in through the accessories. A rug or an accent chair are a good way to include a dash of this strong colour.

VIOLET

And so we reach the end of the rainbow. Richard Of York Has Given Battle in Vain and we have arrived at violet, the seventh colour and the most rarely seen of the seven. But last never did mean least, and violet is full of as much meaning and significance as the rest of the spectrum.

Much was made in November 2016 of Hillary Clinton's concession speech. The defeated Democrat candidate emerged the day after the election wearing a purple pant suit, while Bill stood sadly behind her in a matching tie. The commentators all remarked on this choice of colour. It was, said some, midway between red and blue – did she choose it to indicate that it was time for a compromise between Republican and Democrat? Others said it was a nod to those swing states that she so fatally failed to turn blue – they are also known as the purple states. Or was it a call for unity? *Vanity Fair* magazine suggested it had more to do with the Suffragette movement, or perhaps the Methodists, in whose church Clinton was raised, who believe purple is the colour of penitence. In 1913, the National Women's Party adopted the colours of purple, white and gold, saying that purple represented 'loyalty, constancy to purpose, unswerving steadfastness to a cause'.

It is more traditionally known as the colour of royalty, and these associations date back thousands of years. It was the first man-made dye, and Tyrian purple – made from the secretions of sea snails – may have been used by the Phoenicians as far back as 1570 BC. Phoenicia means 'land of purple' and the colour was highly prized because it did not fade like other shades, but instead became brighter in the sunlight. It was expensive to produce, so purple naturally became associated with the wealthy. It was later restricted for the use of imperial silks only.

In Tudor times only the Royal Family was allowed to wear purple as part of the sumptuary laws, which dated back to Byzantine times and dictated what you could wear according to your position in society. Henry VIII changed the laws several times during his reign, regarding them as a way to maintain the natural hierarchy of society. By the time his daughter Elizabeth I came to the throne, the most expensive of all fabrics, purple velvet, was restricted to the monarch only.

But as with so many colours, the meaning changes according to where in the world you find it. So, in Tudor Britain, violet was also the colour of mourning, while in the modern-day US, the Purple Heart medal denotes courage and honours those who have been wounded in action. In Thailand it is worn by widows mourning their husbands and in Japan it denotes status and wealth. In religious traditions, the purple amethyst is said to be sacred to Buddha, while in Christianity priests wear purple vestments to signify the spirit of reconciliation during Advent and Lent.

Psychologically, purple is the colour of spirituality and is said to encourage creativity as well as calming the mind and nerves. On the flip side, it represents decadence and pomposity.

When it comes to interiors, it's no surprise to learn that purple brings a sense of luxury to a space. It pairs well with other jewel tones such as jade, gold and ruby red and, if used sparingly, can create a feeling of luxury. In its palest incarnation, lavender, it is a cool, relaxing colour that evokes the French countryside; but at the other extreme, aubergine, it is dark and mysterious and perhaps best kept to accents, otherwise it may overwhelm the space and create a rather intense atmosphere.

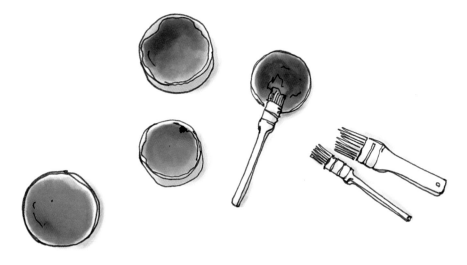

BLACK We may have come to the end of the rainbow, but no exploration of the colour spectrum would be complete without the non-colours, black and white, which are so crucial to creating all the other shades.

First up, black: traditionally associated with mourning and magic, evil and elegance, black is the shade of mystery and secrecy. It is formed by the absorption of all colour and the absence of light. When we wear black we are said to be hiding from ourselves, our weight or perhaps our feelings. But for fashion editors it is practically *de rigueur* to wear this colour at all times, even, or perhaps especially, while telling everyone else to wear pink and yellow. The designer Yohji Yamamoto once said: 'Black is modest and arrogant at the same time. Black is lazy and easy – but mysterious. But above all black says this: I don't bother you – don't bother me.' Steve Jobs was rarely seen in anything other than his signature black polo neck. Audrey Hepburn's LBD (little black dress) in *Breakfast at Tiffany's* made her one of the most instantly recognisable actors in the world.

Black was first worn in the fourteenth century with the emergence of black dye, and since sumptuary laws stated that only the nobility were allowed to wear rich reds and blues, bankers, merchants and government officials started to dress in black clothes made from expensive fabrics instead. Then the nobility copied them. By the end of the sixteenth century it was worn by most of the European monarchy. Since then, black has become the fashion classic, worn by everyone from romantics to poets, punks and goths. But, unlike most of the other colours, it has taken a long time to make its way to interiors.

It has long been said that what you see on the catwalk will end up on cushions, and the time lapse between those two events has become shorter; when recent catwalks showed platforms, suede and 70s-inspired clothes, within weeks the homewares stores were full of macramé plant holders, wall hangings and cork and rattan furniture.

However, black, which has been sashaying down the runways for years, has been the one shade that has been slow to transition to our homes. Yes, it's been a staple of nightclubs and smoky bars, and perhaps the odd teenage bedroom, for decades, signifying the transition from brightly coloured baby room to adulthood. But no-one else dared to paint their walls black unless they were making a real statement. That has finally changed. Dark neutral colours are taking their place alongside the pale ones and it is no longer unusual to see a black wall or black kitchen cupboards. In fact, it is positively fashionable.

Used correctly, black can bring sophistication and drama to a scheme and acts as the perfect backdrop to any works of art and furniture that sit against it. If painting whole walls seems too much, use black in smaller accents. Every room needs some black in it; it provides an anchor for everything else. In a room of pale pastels it stops it looking too sugary sweet. Black is the squeeze of lemon over your food that brings it all to life.

The key to making black work is lots of lighting – wall, floor, table and task lights and mirrors to bounce light around and reflect it back into and from the shadows. You also need to bring in lots of different textures and a combination of matte and shiny surfaces to really make it work.

Using black in interiors will never be a mainstream choice, but it can be the perfect finishing touch to a space. And there is one great place to use it: the wall behind the television, which makes it disappear when it's not turned on, and creates a cinematic effect when it is.

WHITE If black is the absorption of all light, then white, its polar opposite, is the reflection of it all: the sum of all colours. It is, according to many people, the colour of perfection, virginity, innocence and purity and, of course, cleanliness. When it comes to interiors, many of us start off with a coat of white paint everywhere, thinking that we'll leave it as a blank canvas and add some colour later, although often we never get round to it. It's the decorating equivalent of wiping the slate clean – literally painting out the previous occupants' tastes while we wait to uncover the personality of the home we have just moved into.

This means waiting to see how the light flows through the rooms as the day goes on. Learning where the dark corners are and the shadows cast by alcoves and angles. It's the blank page that will be filled not with words and pictures, but with colours and furniture. Ironically, while white is the colour of cleanliness when it comes to clothes, when you put it on your walls it quickly turns to dirtiness, since every scuff and scratch mark will show. So you may end up feeling rather negative about your positive white space.

Very few of us have an all-white house, although there are always exceptions. The home of Chrissie Rucker, founder of London-based interiors store The White Company, is one that springs immediately to mind. The way to do it, so that it doesn't look like a sterile unit in a hospital, is textures and layers. Done well, an all-white room can be stunning, as long as you are slightly loose about what constitutes white. Natural sheepskin rugs, soft rugs and knitted cushions will all create a calm yet welcoming space. Include lots of natural wood for a warm environment and compare how different it might feel if you had a glass coffee table instead. Bring in all the whites from chalk to ivory and make sure the children, turmeric and red wine are kept well away.

White and some pale greys are popular colours in the Scandinavian and Nordic countries because of their long, dark winters. White works equally well in a light and bright room where the white will reflect back on itself and increase the sense of light and space.

Beware, though, of using white in a small, dark room. With no natural light to bounce off, white becomes drab. You will simply have created a small, dark room in a slightly dingy shade of white, not the illusion of space. You will not have made this space feel welcoming. The best solution for that kind of room is to embrace its darkness and paint it in a strong colour. If you really can't bring yourself to do that, use a pale colour, but the key word is colour. Anything that isn't white, so a soft grey, a gentle green or a delicate blue. Paint the ceiling the same colour to make it seem higher and blur the edges. You can add white furniture if you want, but that brings us back to that welcoming thing again. How welcome do people feel in a room with white sofas? I always think that, while it might look stunning in a photograph, it's a slightly hostile act. Sure, come into my house, but make sure you're clean. Don't spill your drink and leave your shoes carefully by the door. It's not a house that says come on in, kick off your shoes and grab a drink, is it? And that thought brings us to the hall, which is effectively where your home greets people.

1

THE
HALL

The hall is the first thing you see when you enter someone's home. Make it count, because it sets the tone for everything else. In a house, it leads you to the stairs, which are the backbone of the building. Yet halls and stairs are often the most neglected parts of our homes: with its poor lighting, bad storage, bikes, bags and boots, the hall is often the one place we can't wait to get out of. We rush through, throwing our possessions aside to get to the well-lit sanctuary of a room we have spent time, and money, decorating.

But hold on a minute. Remember that job interview training where they went on and on about first impressions? Would you turn up to meet a prospective employer with unwashed hair, and spinach in your teeth? The hall is arguably the most important room of the house. It is certainly the hardest working. It has to fit all that storage into a comparatively small space, make you feel welcome and give a hint as to what one might expect from the rest of the rooms. So the hall needs to be fun and welcoming, practical and attractive.

When you open the door after a hard day's work or a business trip, or get back from the supermarket with supper in a bag, the hall needs to say: 'Come on in, I've been waiting for you, let me take your coat. Now put your shoes here, and your keys there. That's better, why don't you go through to the kitchen and find a drink and a comfortable chair.' Is your hall saying that to you?

Or is it shouting: 'Where the hell have you been, what do you think you're doing, trying to stick your coat on top of the 15 that are already crammed on to that hook? Well of course you've tripped over the shoes, and bruised your leg on the bike! Look, just stick your bag on the handlebars. Now go on, get out of the way, there's no room for you here.' If that sounds familiar, come with me.

THE WALLS

Unless you live in some vast country house or detached Victorian villa, the chances are your hall is smaller and darker than you'd like. So let's get the first point out of the way. You either already have, or were planning to, paint it white. But for white to do its job of bouncing light around and making the space feel bigger and brighter, it needs some natural light to reflect back on itself and to create more light. If you don't have that – and many halls don't have windows – then all you have is a small, dark space that you have painted white. In these situations the paint will take on a slightly drab air, as if it knew what is was supposed to be doing but couldn't quite summon up the energy for it.

If you live in a rental and aren't allowed to paint the walls, the mirror is your friend. Try and angle it so that it can reflect the light from the rooms that lead off it and bounce it back into the hall. Or arrange a collection of mirrors in different shapes and sizes to create a gallery effect. If you can paint the walls, get the colour charts out. The point of the hall is that no-one lingers there, however welcoming it is, so you can afford to be dramatic and daring.

Painting it a dark colour will make the other rooms leading off it seem brighter. It will make a statement and, from a practical point of view, it won't show the inevitable scuff marks from all those hands, bags, boots and bikes. Think navy blue, dark green or charcoal. All of these work in artificial light as well as daylight and you can add a couple of large mirrors as mentioned above. The difference is that now it looks like you meant it. You have embraced that small dark hall and made a feature of its size and lack of natural light. If you're feeling really brave, take the dark paint over the doors, architraves and skirting boards. (You don't have to paint both sides of the door the same colour, so don't worry about that.)

If this feels like a step too far, consider the half-painted wall. When you paint two different colours above and below a picture rail it looks traditional. If you don't have a picture rail, but divide the wall in half anyway, it looks really modern. It also looks as though you've thought about it and made a decision, rather than just slapping some paint on the wall. It looks, to coin an interior designer's phrase, 'considered'.

And, before you ask – the stairs? Well, you can take the dark paint up the wall opposite the bannisters and stop at the top; then you can carry on round in a paler colour if you don't

want to go dark all the way up. Or you can make the landing walls half and half so that there is some continuity with the hall but it's not all as dark.

There is one more place you can paint to add a little personality: the back of the front door. I have a client who has painted her hallway dark grey but the back of the door is a zinging yellow and it looks fantastic. It brings in some light and adds lots of character. I have painted mine in a burgundy shade, which goes with the stairs opposite and stops it being a complete white-out. Sadly, my hall is too small for furniture of any kind so the paint has to do all the work of making an impact.

Another trick, which I saw in a house in Portugal, is to tile the bottom half of the wall. This makes it tough, wipe-clean and beautiful. Finish it off with edging tiles. In a bathroom, these will look old-fashioned and a bit 1980s – because that's the traditional place to put them – but in a hall they will look contemporary and cool, mainly because it's a bit more unexpected.

Now that the walls are looking a bit more interesting, it's time to think about the floor.

THE FLOOR

Practical flooring is an absolute must for the hall – and I write as someone who has white painted floorboards. Let me explain. In our old house, with two boys under the age of eight, we chose a pinkish slate for the hall floor. This led to a sort of milk chocolate-coloured carpet that ran all the way up the stairs to the top of the house. It was basically mud coloured. Indisputably practical as a choice for a family of boys, you might say. But when something doesn't show the dirt it's quite hard to persuade yourself to clean it. I'm pretty sure that floor was filthy.

Now that I have a white floor I can see when it's dirty and I clean it. Mind you, my sons are not football players and someone (it wasn't me) has taught them and all their friends to take their shoes off as soon as they have closed the front door.

For those of you with putative sporting heroes, dogs, bikes and a dislike of dirty floors, you need something you can mop, sweep and vacuum.

Floorboards and tiles are the best options, but if you live in a first floor flat where hard floors have been banned to save the ears of the neighbours below, then dark carpet is your friend, and – now don't panic – patterned carpet is even better.

Patterned carpet has come a long way since the pubs of the 1970s. These days you can find lots of black and white geometric patterns, for example, that look great and won't show the dirt. If that still makes you nervous, lay a long strip of carpet as a runner and nail down the edges with gold upholstery pins (I am indebted to Bianca Hall, author of the French for Pineapple interiors blog, for that idea) so that it won't be a trip hazard.

Once you've sorted out the hall floor, many of you will be eyeing the stairs. This is another opportunity to have fun. The stairs are usually the first thing a guest will see, and they're probably one of the first things you see when you come home at the end of the day. Don't buy that sensible oatmeal twist. Whose heart ever started to beat faster at the sight of a neutral carpet? It's the equivalent of magnolia, and it's boring. And it isn't all that practical either, because it will show the dirt – mostly the mud and pale dog hairs.

My stairs are spotty. A deep burgundy with large ivory spots. They truly make my heart sing every time I come home. You can have stripes or flowers if you prefer. I have a friend whose hall is tiled with a black, grey and white flower pattern leading to an emerald green stair runner. The sides of the stairs are painted black to chime with the hall floor tiles and it looks fantastic.

Another trick, recommended by interiors journalist Jo Leevers, is to buy a series of cheap kilim runners from the high street and nail them up the stairs. I once visited the house of a jewellery designer who had fixed pieces of leather to her stairs that she had bought as offcuts. It's fantastically practical, as it's completely non-slip and looks better with age, but it's also incredibly luxe. It will last forever too, and that's another point worth making. My grandmother always cautioned me against velvet curtains: 'They'll never wear out, dear, and you'll never have an excuse for new ones.' So, think carefully about the leather stair runner because you might have it for a while. Mind you, on the upside, the moths won't want to eat it; I speak as someone who lost several steps to the munching marauders in a previous house.

The hall is arguably the most important room in the house. It's certainly the first place that anyone sees and, as such, sets the tone for the rest. It needs to be both welcoming and fun, practical and pretty. This space needs to be able to greet you at the end of a hard day and give you somewhere to hang your coat. But it can also be dramatic as it's a space that you simply pass through en route to somewhere else. You can afford to be bold with your decorating choices here.

THE LIGHTING

As with the floors and walls, don't waste the opportunity to show a bit of your personality when it comes to the lighting. Yes, you can have downlights (yawn) but they're so boring and the light is so intense. Frankly, all you need to do in the hall is make sure that your shoes match and that your lipstick isn't all over your teeth – you're not doing open heart surgery in there.

If you've got the ceiling height, the hall is the place for a showstopper light: maybe a chandelier made of wooden beads, a pendant lamp made from feathers (you can aim the hairdryer at it to clean it), something made from brass or silver to catch the eye and bounce the light around the space, reflecting itself in that mirror you'll be hanging on the wall.

I give those two examples of lights deliberately. It's always a good trick to use materials in unexpected ways.

The advent of LEDs that don't heat up has freed up lighting designers to use all sorts of materials that used to be too dangerous for the heat of a tungsten bulb; now you can use recycled cardboard, knitted lights, the aforementioned feathers. Have fun. As I say, you're not reading annual reports in there, and if you need to remove a splinter, go to the bathroom. Another good lighting trick is neon. These days, you can have anything made in neon that you can afford to pay for. It will add a little ambient light and fun to a small space. In short, the hall is a room like any other. It needs designing and thinking about just as much as the kitchen and the bedroom.

THE STORAGE

There are very few halls that can store everything you want. Sooner or later, a little discipline is going to have to come into play: the summer jackets cannot live there in the depths of winter and the quilted parkas need to go upstairs when it's 30 degrees outside.

That said, there needs to be a minimum of one coat hook per person and a space for shoes, bags and brollies. There is a school of thought that keys should never live in the hall as it's a security risk, so you might as well get into the habit of putting them in the kitchen. In our house we have the Drawer. This is the drawer into which my dearly beloved tips his keys, headphones, travel card, loose change and receipts at the end of the day. Before I invented this drawer it ended up in a pile on the kitchen worktop, which grew ever larger as the week went on until, by Saturday morning, it had eaten everything else. In an ideal world we would each have a Drawer, but our kitchen didn't quite pan out like that. It works on a needs-must basis and I have my handbag to collect stuff in. If you can have one drawer per person, try to do that; you'll be so grateful for this as time goes by.

Back to the hall. You don't have to hang the hooks in a straight line. There's an enormous choice of hooks

out there and some of them are fabulous. Arrange them on the wall in a random pattern, with the lowest one a jacket height from the floor. That way, even when they're empty (unlikely I know), it looks like a decorative feature. Another feature, which we also have in the kitchen but which would work well in the hall, is the personalised mail box. Buy one of those wall-mounted wire baskets for each member of the family (adding names is optional). Then each person has a place for their post – both incoming or outgoing – or the homework that needs to go out of the door the following day. It's a good way to store the week's admin that piles up and forces you to sort it out before the next lot comes in. It also, crucially, stops piles of clutter building up on the precious kitchen worktop.

Shoe storage is the bane of many a hall, as there are always too many, and chucking them into a basket might be fine for trainers but is an early grave for anything precious. If you don't have a hideous radiator all along the wall (*sobs*), why not build two shelves, as long as they can possibly be? Make sure the top one is strong enough and wide enough to sit on, then put shoes on the bottom one. Bingo – shoe storage and a seat at the same time. If you don't need to sit there you can put a plant on

it and make it look decorative instead. The key to these shelves is that they must be fixed to the wall, not the floor. The more floor you can see, the bigger the space will appear. A floating shelf with shoes on it will keep the floor clear so your hall instantly feels tidier and less cluttered.

ANY OTHER FURNITURE

I appreciate that most of you won't be reading this part. I wouldn't if I wasn't writing it; my hall has a radiator and a mirror in it. There's no room for anything else. But wait – if I'd had underfloor heating, there would have been. When we did this house up there was no money for underfloor heating. The plumber urged us to reconsider. 'You'll regret it,' he said. 'I'll do you a deal.' But there was no deal to be done – we had rewiring and new windows to pay for and there was nothing left in the pot to rip up the floorboards and install the heating underfoot.

Six years on, and I hate that radiator. Without it, we might just have had room for a row of vintage folding cinema seats, one for everyone to sit and put their shoes on. Without it, we could have squeezed in a narrow console table for a bunch of flowers and couple of candlesticks. But we have it, and it's staying. While I'm on the subject, you can't have a radiator cover. What is the point of trying to pretend that it isn't a radiator? It's there and it's doing its job – don't make it harder for it to spread its heat. If you need to have a radiator there, think about replacing it with a more stylish one. They come in all sorts of shapes and colours these days, so make a feature of it rather than trying to pretend it isn't there.

Still, that's my hall. You may have space for a dedicated flower table. Or a chair and a small lamp that you can have on a timer so that it's lit when you come home on dark winter evenings. A wooden church pew with storage is great for those who have the room. Wellies inside, bags on top, job done. In short, if you have room for any furniture in your hall, make sure it is doing at least two jobs – storing and seating, for example. Oh, and a third: looking good. What better room to invoke William Morris's interiors maxim: 'Have nothing in your houses that you do not know to be useful or believe to be beautiful.'

2

THE KITCHEN

When I'm asked to help someone with their kitchen, very often the first thing that becomes apparent is that they're working either to their architect's vision or to their own idealised vision of what the perfect kitchen should be, rather than the one they actually want or need. They are dreaming of that sunshine-filled room from the TV ads with the perfect children sitting round the perfectly laid table eating with perfect manners and chatting politely while Dad reads the paper and Mum hovers by the stove smiling beatifically. The reality is four or five people rushing in and out swearing and dropping things, then spilling coffee on someone's homework while the dog steals the toast and the cat quietly drops a mouse on the floor and lurks silently, waiting for the shriek that will surely follow.

Now, while it might not yet be possible to design a room that can teach your children perfect manners, you can create one that will encourage conversation. A kitchen that is easy to move around with well-organised storage. You need to make your kitchen work for you and your family, by which I mean the people who actually live there, not for that lot off the telly who came in from central casting. If you hate cooking, don't shell out on a huge range cooker. If your oven doubles up as shoe storage, don't spend a fortune on it. If, on the other hand, you're that person who is always in the kitchen at parties, make sure you create a space to cater for that: bar stools and a wine fridge, a hob that faces into the room so that you don't have your back to everyone when you're whipping up a few canapés.

This is one of the most important questions to ask when it comes to designing a room (any room): who's going to use and it and what will they be doing there? It might seem obvious, but making toast and heating up a ready-meal is a far cry from making your own pasta and icing cakes. *To thine own self be true* goes the saying and, just as you know you shouldn't buy that dress in the sale on a promise that you will slim down into it, don't assume that a fabulous kitchen with all mod cons is going to turn you into Nigella Lawson or Anthony Bourdain.

HOW TO PLAN
THE PERFECT KITCHEN LAYOUT

At first it might seem overwhelming trying to plan the perfect kitchen, but the chances are you've already worked out what's annoying you about your current one, so you might as well use that as a starting point and begin by thinking how you could put those issues right. In other words, before you start obsessing about what you do want, the kitchen is the one room where it really pays to know what you *don't* want. That is, how to get the layout right; because this is the room where planning really is everything. Chances are that in the sitting room the TV point is already there, and there may be only one place where the sofa fits, so you have to work around that. But when you redo the kitchen you're free to choose whether you want the dishwasher to the left or right of the sink. Where to put the fridge. Are you going to store the pans there? Or over there? And what about the mugs?

Sometimes it's simply a question of changing those ugly cupboard doors for more contemporary ones. You can make a huge difference simply by changing the handles. More commonly, it's about not having enough storage or worktop space. If that's the case, you need to start by having a really good clear-out to see what rubbish (I mean stuff that you don't use) you've been hanging on to for years. Sort that out and you will see how much extra cupboard space you already have.

We all know that if the fancy utensils live in the cupboard, that's where they stay. Hands up who's got a juicer in the cupboard? Hands up who uses it? Thought so. I'm guessing that those of you who decided to make room for it on the worktop are getting a lot more use out of it. The rest of you? Take it to the charity shop and free up the space. It's a good idea to invite a friend who likes cooking round to use your kitchen and cast a pair of fresh eyes on your set-up. They are more likely to notice if the pans are miles away from the hob and the chopping boards are inaccessible, things you've become so used to that you no longer notice. Ask them to tell you the truth, and listen to what they say.

Start by making a list of what you want your kitchen to be. You need to write down the first thing that comes into your head. Is it the heart of the home or a place to cook? Family hangout or entertaining space? These things will help you decide if you are creating a social kitchen where everyone will gather, or a practical room that is purely about function. It's not all dictated by the size, either. You might want a relatively small kitchen

area (by which I mean cooking, washing and preparation) so you can fit a large table for everyone to sit around. Or you might be dreaming of an island where friends will perch on stools and chat while you cook. If it's a large room, do you want a big table or a squashy sofa? You need to know how you're going to use the room before you start fantasising about marble worktops and vintage bar stools.

What about that fabled triangle that kitchen fitters are always recommending? Fifty years ago, efficiency experts tracked the average woman's steps in the kitchen and found

a natural pathway between the fridge, cooker and sink, hence the triangle. The distance between those three items and how easy it is to reach them is still sometimes used as a measure of the perfect kitchen today, but you don't have to be bound by it. Unless your kitchen is enormous, you're not going to wear yourself out taking a few extra steps to the fridge if that is the best, or only, place for it.

It's a complex equation to work out the optimal measurements but, basically, the sides of the triangle don't have to be equal, as long as the distances add up to somewhere between 3.5m

continued >>>

THE PERFECT KITCHEN LAYOUT *continued* >>>

and 7m. So, if the cooker and fridge are 1m apart, the sink and fridge could be 2.5m apart and the cooker and sink 3m apart. Clearly, there is room for flexibility. Quite often you'll find that you instinctively know how it should be because it feels comfortable, and I would go with that rather than tying yourself in knots doing sums.

There is, however, one measurement which I think does make a difference. If you're having a kitchen island, there should be at least 1.2m between it and the nearest counter, according to the experts. In my kitchen we have 1.1m, mainly because there wasn't enough space for more but, by a happy accident, it turns out that for me (1.7m tall) that is exactly the right distance to pivot from worktop to hob and back again without having to take a step. Any wider and I would have to take a small step; not exactly hard work, but pivoting is easier. Try it and see; then try it with a heavy pan of boiled potatoes. If there's no room for an island, you might be able to squeeze in a peninsula – an island that is attached to the cupboards at one end, creating an L-shape. While we're doing measurements, you really do need 1m clear at either end to make it comfortable to walk past. At a push, 80cm will do, but that's tight

(an internal door is around 76cm wide, for comparison) and you don't want everything to feel squashed.

The big issue for any kitchen is storage. Open-plan shelving is very fashionable, but some people worry about the dust and splashing from the hob. I have shelves, but they are positioned away from the hob. In general, I find that the things I use all the time – plates, glasses, cooking oils and so on, don't get dusty – but the champagne flutes on the top shelf do tend to need a rinse before using. I can live with that. You might not want to.

If you want wall-mounted cupboards, make sure they extend all the way up to the ceiling, which will make the ceiling look higher. If the cupboards stop short of the ceiling you'll inevitably store things on top of them, but since you can't reach them without a stool you won't use them, so they will get dusty and make the space look cluttered. A tall cupboard means you can store them out of sight and keep the room looking clearer and more spacious.

It's worth noting that, like electrical sockets, you always need more storage than you think. And, like planning a wardrobe, don't assume that what you have now is all you will ever have. I was once sent a very fancy mixer to review. My cupboards were so full it literally had to live on the floor until I gave in and took it to the charity shop. Calculate how many cupboards you need for the stuff you have – the things you actually use – and try and squeeze in a couple more for the stuff you don't need very often, and the things you'll buy in the future.

Once you have done the planning, think about the appliances. Big brand names can add resale value and you should always, always, buy the best you can afford. But this is where the type of kitchen you need versus the type of kitchen you want really comes into play. A range cooker is sexy and attractive, but if you cook a lot and have back problems, you might be better off with an eye-level one. That American fridge you've been dreaming of will take up a huge amount of space and it's an unwritten law that you will fill the top shelf with sauces that you buy for one recipe and never touch again. We had an under-counter fridge for many years and, while it was irritating during family holidays or when catering for parties, most of the time it was fine. It also forced us to plan menus and shop responsibly because there was no room for stuff we weren't going to eat. Now we have a bigger kitchen and a bigger fridge and, yes, we probably waste a little more food.

Americans are often appalled that in the UK so many of us have the washing machine in the kitchen. So, apparently, are the British upper classes, but they are probably also aghast that the rest of us don't have staff to do said laundry. Can you squeeze it in somewhere else to make room for another cupboard or a dishwasher?

Think it through. All of it. This is the room that will take most of your money, and the one you're least likely to change later, so it's worth spending a little more time on the details. Can the kids reach their own cereal so you can have a lie-in at the weekend? Is the bread bin near the toaster? Is there room for the mugs near the coffee machine? I can unload my dishwasher and put everything away with only one pivot. Since I hate unloading the dishwasher, this is perfect for me; you might have other bugbears that good layout can solve. Think it all through.

When we were planning the open shelves in our kitchen, I drew a diagram and worked out exactly what I wanted to store on them and where it would go. Over the last eight years we have often dreamed of replacing our budget units (Swedish, since you ask) with something more bespoke, but we wouldn't change the layout. We thought it all through.

CHOOSING **WORKTOPS** AND **SPLASHBACKS**

When it comes to worktops, gone are the days when you were being quite posh if you chose wood and announcing your wealth if you ran to granite – but then, like most people, you just selected the right shade of laminate and forgot about it. These days, if you're looking to create your dream kitchen, you can choose from dozens of different materials, including stone, quartz composites, Corian and slate, not forgetting those old favourites, wood and stainless steel. But how do they all stack up in terms of practicality? Wood is warm to the touch and very natural, but there are negatives. It burns, it's porous and you have re-seal it every few months. It will collect water if it's near an under-mounted sink and turn black and mouldy.

White Carrara marble is on many a wishlist, but it's touchy stuff. It's porous, so you need to be careful if you're hurling turmeric, tomato purée or red wine about. I know one high-end interior designer who says it's wonderful but she neither cooks nor has children, so it's about being decorative. Of course, if, like me, you feel that a bit of staining adds patina and character, go ahead. But not everyone sees it that way.

Granite is more practical, but again it needs properly sealing and if you

drop a glass it won't bounce. The composites are tough and look good, but use a trivet before you put a hot pan down on them.

For every worktop pro there is a con, and so it's worth considering a mix of surfaces. Think in zones. Wood for the eating area, Corian for the sink and food prep and perhaps granite around the cooker where it needs to withstand hot pans. As for me, I have stainless steel. It can take the abuse of hot pans, water and scratches without making a fuss. Yes, it is quite an industrial look, but we have softened it with leather handles on the cupboards and reclaimed painted floorboards that are an antidote to the cool modernity of the steel. And basically, if it's good enough for a professional restaurant it's good enough for me. I would be more distressed by black mould around the sink on a wooden counter, or a half moon lemon stain on the marble. You have to decide where to compromise. Because here's the thing: the estate agent might tell you it's location, location, location but I'm afraid, unless you are a squillionaire, that it's actually compromise, compromise, compromise.

Now, by the time you've factored in all the appliances, the worktop and all the other hardware, the kitchen often ends up being full of hard surfaces and straight lines. One antidote is to introduce some pattern in the splashback. We're not talking those old-fashioned tiles with a random teapot in one corner and a pomegranate in another. Think encaustic, Delft or geometric designs. Lay plain metro tiles in a brick or herringbone formation and add coloured grout. In short: have some fun. This is a room you are going to be in every single day. It needs to reflect your personality and make you happy.

Another option is a large piece of foxed mirror. This has the dark spots and smokiness of antique mirror, so your kitchen won't look like a gym, but it will also reflect the light and bounce it back out into the room. It's a little bit unusual, too, which is always a good thing. You can also fit it at the base of the cupboards instead of a traditional wooden kickboard. It will reflect the floor and make the cupboards look as if they are floating.

Or what about glass? These days you can have glass in any colour you care

to mention – all you've got to do is pick one. One advantage of glass is that you can write on it with a whiteboard pen and it will rub off easily. This is handy for shopping lists and reminders and may save you from writing, as my mother once did, 'eggs' in toothpaste on the bathroom mirror to remind my grandmother to go shopping. She used a whole tube of toothpaste, so my grandmother had to buy that, too. Fortunately we didn't need aubergines.

This is the room, perhaps more than any other, that you need to plan in detail. And you need to design the kitchen for who you really are not who you think you want to be. If you don't cook then don't spend a fortune on a fancy range cooker. It is a space where you can be inventive to create storage and seating that works for you.

GETTING KITCHEN LIGHTING RIGHT

Lighting is so tricky. We're constantly told we need to plan it before the room has been built, yet it's so hard to imagine exactly what we'll want before we have a room to put it in. I worked with Sally Storey, the design director of John Cullen Lighting in London, who regularly holds masterclasses on this very subject and who came to my house to point out what I had got right (not so much) and where I had gone wrong (so much more).

One of the first things to emerge is that you don't need to have a regimented grid of spotlights marching along the kitchen ceiling. This is what builders love and will automatically do if you don't keep a close eye on them. You need to decide instead where you actually need the lights and place them accordingly, the point being that if they are properly installed you should barely see the lights themselves, merely the illumination that they provide. Basically, you shouldn't be looking up at the ceiling – unless you're trying to swat a fly – so it doesn't matter about having a symmetrical pattern.

Most of us don't buy properly recessed downlights, either. This means we end up with the bulb flush with the ceiling, which means you see both the bulb and a harsh light around it, rather than just being generally aware of light in the place where you need it. So that's the second tip: if you're having downlights, make sure you buy ones with a bulb that can be recessed back into the ceiling. Ideally this bulb should have a black baffle (the trim that surrounds the bulb) around it to reduce the glare. It might sound counter-intuitive in a white ceiling, but a white surround will reflect the light from the bulb back out, making you more aware of it. A black one will absorb the immediate harshness of the bulb light and refract back only the soft light that you need to see by.

The next issue is one of atmosphere. It can be hard to create this in kitchens, when most of us just use those downlights. Rule number 1: have dimmers in every room and put the lights on different circuits, so you can have light over the islands for cooking but turn them off to hide the washing up when you're eating at the table or breakfast bar.

Even though it's the kitchen, it's not just about spotlights. Try to include a table lamp for a soft ambient light, or a wall light if you don't have worktop space. If you have enough ceiling

continued >>>

height, a row of pendant lights over the island or table is always a winner. Try hanging three of the same lights in different colours, or three of the same colour at different heights, or three different lights in the same colour. You get the idea. If you want glass lights, choose interesting bulbs – there's no shortage of those around these days.

Another tip is LED tape, which is basically like clever Sellotape with bulbs in. Fix it under open shelves to highlight what is on them. I have a skylight in my kitchen, which isn't lit at all. Sally suggested hollowing out a groove around the inside edge and installing LED tape so that the tiny bulbs are hidden from view but the ambient light remains. Suddenly, it becomes possible to light an entire

kitchen without using spotlights at all. Not that you'll want to, as they are useful in the prep area, but don't assume that's all you need or can have in this room.

Finally, don't forget the outside space, if you have it. A couple of lights in the garden or on the decking will throw a soft light back into the dining end of the kitchen, as well as softly illuminating the world outside, which is better than just a deep black nothing on the other side of the glass.

KITCHEN LIGHTING: A CHECKLIST

☐ Don't put your spotlights in a symmetrical grid.

☐ Make sure your spotlights are fully recessed into the ceiling.

☐ Always install dimmer switches.

☐ Have the lights on two or three different circuits so you can choose which part of the room to light.

☐ Consider wall, table and pendant lights in every room – including the kitchen.

☐ Think about imaginative use of LED tape.

☐ Don't forget the outside space.

THE KITCHEN FLOOR

I'm often asked to help people find material for their kitchen floor that can carry on to the outside and blend in seamlessly with the patio. To which the short answer is, why? It's all very well linking the two spaces, but the chances are that you'll end up with grey tiles both inside and out, which will look like a pavement outside and be cold inside.

I'm also often asked this by people who have vast kitchens, or will have by the time the glass doors to the patio have gone in. I can see a case for it if the kitchen is small and you want to trick the eye into thinking the space is bigger than it is, but mostly you end up with a giant compromise in that neither area has the ideal flooring. Matching the two is one of those clichéd design ideas that probably came off the telly and doesn't really work for anyone.

It's far better to decide what you want inside and then – clever, this – decide what you want outside and, as long as the two don't clash completely, it will look great. After all, just because the outside looks the same as inside it doesn't actually make your kitchen bigger. Most of the time (in the UK, at any rate), you'll be looking at it through a pane of glass. And while I'm making controversial statements, here's another: I have never, ever, seen

a plain grey-tiled kitchen floor that didn't look cold, municipal and boring.

If wooden floorboards aren't practical for you – they can stain and be draughty – think about tiles that look like wood. These days it's practically impossible to tell the difference and if you have underfloor heating and they're warm to touch, who cares if they're ceramic or not? You can choose from parquet or boards or even distressed ones that look like reclaimed floorboards. If you want to create a link with the outside, buy some garden furniture the same colour as the kitchen cupboards and link the space that way.

I had one client who thought about patterned floor tiles but, in the end, opted for safe grey. Her garden was small and she had a large glass table in the kitchen that was a rather beautiful aquamarine colour. I suggested she paint the rendered wall at the end of the garden in a shade to match the table, and the concrete bench that had been constructed at the bottom of the wall in a darker version of the same shade. At a stroke, she had united inside and outside spaces and warmed up those grey floor tiles. Inside and outside were also perfectly linked by colour instead of material.

Tiles will always be the most practical choice in a kitchen, as they are easy to clean and can be heated; but since kitchens are full of straight lines and hard surfaces, pattern is rare. Patterned tiles will soften the space, but if the whole floor seems too much, why not do part of it? Perhaps in the shape of a rug under the table, or fixed at an angle to 'bleed' into a wooden floor or plain tiles.

THE SPECIAL TREAT

We all need one, and no, it's not José Mourinho. If you're doing up the kitchen, think of the one treat gadget you would like and see if you can factor it into the budget. Mine is my boiling water tap. A friend of mine wanted a steam oven way before they were fashionable. Maybe you would like a TV on the fridge door, or a fridge which incorporates a smaller door so you can just reach in and grab the milk. How about an extractor hood that looks like a chandelier? Don't forget a slimline wine fridge that will slide into an awkward space. Or what about a barbecue grill indoors? Although, if that's your bag, you'd better factor in a state-of-the-art extractor fan as well.

Cooking is not a daily joy for many, yet most of us have to do it at some point or another. Work out what will make it easier and more enjoyable (or perhaps less detestable) and see if you can afford it. You may have to compromise on another element, but maybe you're prepared to do that. I wanted trench heating in the kitchen; I also wanted a boiling water tap. I have a bog-standard radiator, and I can live with that.

3

THE
DINING
ROOM

The formal dining room may be out of fashion but, like Arnie, it will be back. In the meantime, most of us have created an eating area at one end of the kitchen or sitting room. It doesn't matter if you have a separate room or use the corner of another one, you still need to consider this space carefully, as it has a function in its own right.

The French wouldn't dream of eating in the kitchen and, even if they have a lot of space in there, would rather put a dining table in a small sitting room than eat surrounded by pots, pans and washing up. The Italians always want to eat at a table, even if it's a small folding one that has to be put away after every meal. Also, have you ever been to rural Italian restaurants and wondered why the lighting is so bright and so defiantly overhead? It's because they like to see what they are eating and who they are talking to. The dimly lit romantic restaurant is for cities and foreigners, and possibly those serving bad food (I made that last one up). The Danes, on the other hand, claim to have invented the 'conversation kitchen', as they call it: an open-plan space where the whole family can gather to cook, eat, sit, chat and do homework.

It's often said that the kitchen is the heart of the home, but I think it's the dining table, whichever room you choose to put it in. This is the site of long lunches and late dinners, the place where family gathers and friends are invited. The table is used for homework, for crafting, for admin and eating. For sipping wine and drinking coffee. For family meetings and wedding planning. Your kitchen table represents your life. Choose wisely, as it will bear witness to many things.

CHOOSING THE RIGHT TABLE

It might be a table in the kitchen, or you might have a dedicated dining room. Whichever it is, I think the table around which you and your family and friends gather to eat is one of the most important purchases you'll make. As first-time buyers or those moving into their first flat after leaving home, it might only be a tiny table, but it will always hold memories of that time and may later, in a bigger house, function as a desk or a dressing table.

Our first kitchen table came from my mother's house. It was one of the first things she bought when we moved into our own house after divorcing my father and living with my grandmother for a few years. An antique pine rectangle, she kept it until she could replace it with an antique oak circle, which she felt was more grown up.

It languished in a garage for a few years while I travelled and studied before I finally came to rest in a rented house in Birmingham, where I did my journalism indentures and moved it in with me. Along with my mother's Welsh dresser, which I had also acquired by that stage, it followed me to London and various rental flats. Eventually we bought a bigger table and that one became my son's desk. Once it was covered in felt pen and glitter glue we eventually got rid of it, but it took some of our memories with it when it left.

What shape is best for you? Most of us haven't got room for a square one, but if you do, the rules of the circle apply (see below). Rectangles are the most common, but if you regularly seat six or more people you'll immediately break the conversation into two or three parts. King Arthur didn't have a round table for nothing, you know. If you need flexible seating, consider a bench along one side – you can soften it with sheepskins and cushions and keep chairs at the ends and opposite. That way no-one has to sit on a bench if they don't want to, but if you suddenly find extra teenagers or smalls from a spontaneous playdate demanding food, there's always room to squeeze in another one. A bench also means that you can push the table over the bench and up against the wall when not all the space is needed.

A circular table is better for a small room and better if there are toddlers careering about because they're drawn to sharp corners like dogs to a stick.

But mostly it comes down to preference. Round or rectangle, it doesn't really matter as long as it fits the space. The key thing to know is that ideally you need to allow 1 metre (just over a yard) for a chair to pull out when someone stands up from the table. This also allows someone else to walk behind a seated person. If you want a round table, which is better for conversation and means everyone can reach the pepper – then 1-metre diameter is the minimum for four. Less is doable, but tight. More is better. If you haven't got space for that, consider a round table that will extend to become an oval. Make a rough calculation of 60cm per person; 75cm is better if they have wide elbows. If you have a rectangle and people are sitting at either end, you'll need another 30cm in length.

Now let's talk about legs. Eero Saarinen, the Finnish-American architect and industrial designer, came up with the classic circular Tulip table, which has a single pedestal leg. It was designed, as Saarinen said, to eliminate the 'slum of legs' found under most standard tables when you add chairs. He later created the matching Tulip chair for the same reason. Still in production, despite its ear-bleedingly high price, this style of table remains the best choice for those who prefer a clean, minimal look.

If you have a rectangular table with a leg at each corner – bear with me – this will also appear to take up more space in a room. We had an old art-school table for many years with thick, solid legs. It wasn't until we replaced it with a new one that we realised how much the original had dominated the space. The new one is longer and wider but has two pedestal legs that are tucked in under the table and are much less visible. The whole space instantly appears much bigger and less squashed despite the fact that the table is larger, which makes it instantly more relaxing too. It means that you're more likely to want to sit there. And people wonder why the Danes believe that good design makes you happy!

So four legs good, two not always better, but worth thinking about. Finally, if you fall for a table with fancy legs, you need to pick chairs with simple legs if you're going to avoid the aforementioned slum of legs. The classic Eames Eiffel chair will lose its drama and just look messy under a table with its own complicated standing arrangement.

Finally, don't forget that if you have a circular table with four legs and you intend to seat more than four people, someone's going to have to straddle those legs. Yes, there is a lot to think about, but you probably weren't going to and now that I have, all you need to do is pick the one you like based on the requirements you now know you have.

GETTING THE
LIGHTING RIGHT

Whether it's a corner of the kitchen or a whole room, the lighting in the eating area needs to multi-task. From bright and cheery breakfasts (the décor, if not the diners) to romantic, candlelit suppers, this space needs to work for them all.

The first part is simple: dimmers. I will own up to having totally failed on the dimmer front, so make sure you don't. They are perhaps more crucial in this space than any other, particularly as you might not have space for a table on which to put a lamp, or spare floor for a tall light. Assuming that's the case, it's question of ceiling or wall lights, depending on the height of the former. We have a fairly low (builder's standard) ceiling in our kitchen extension, so pendant lights were not the ideal solution. In addition to this, the table sits in front of glass doors that lead out into the garden and, if we were ever going to move the table out of the way to have a party, we didn't want to be left with dangling lights in the middle of the dance floor. I raise this as people often say that they don't want pendant lights over the table because they might want to move it for parties, but I always want to know where they are moving this table to. Most of us need to dance around or even on the table, rather than being able to move it

to another room. Mind you, if dancing on the table is your plan you don't want to knock yourself out on the chandelier, so you might be better off with wall lights after all.

Wall lights are what we have. There are so many around these days that it's not hard to find cool ones. Again, there are options; mount them high to wash light down the wall, or hide little spot lights in the skirting to flood light up the wall. Think of them as earrings on an outfit – they decorate the wall when both on and off. If pendants are your thing, hang them low over the table. It's much more dramatic and intimate, as long as the lowest one is higher than the head of the tallest person when they're sitting down.

There's a handy trick you can use with pendant lights if you do want to move the table. Ask the electrician to rewire your light with an extra-long flex (you can buy coloured electrical flex easily these days), then install a hook on the ceiling at the edge of the room. When the lights are over the table you can loop the long flex into a circle or loose knot, which – since you have bought it in a pretty colour that picks up on a detail of the room – will look like a great little decorative detail, and then, when the dancing starts, you can simply unloop the flex, stretch the

light to the side and hang it at the edge of the room, far away from bopping heads and dad-dancing arms.

This trick works equally well in a room where the pendant isn't in the right place. For example, in a rental sitting room where you want the light over the dining table in the corner instead of in the middle of the room.

Rather than rewiring the room and moving the ceiling rose – which you might not be allowed to do anyway – you can wire in a light on a long flex, hook it wherever you need it to be and put it back when you move.

Dining rooms are going out of fashion these days as (unlike this one, shot in 1953) everyone rushes to knock down the walls and create an eat-in kitchen. But if you do have a dining room, make sure you decorate it to be fit for purpose and not just as fancy storage for the pushchair and the piles of paperwork. Look for a sideboard to house your crockery, ready to lay the table for guests. As with the hall, you can be bold in here as it's a room that isn't used every day. Perfect for that fabulous wallpaper – do all four walls please – or a dramatic pendant light hung low over the table.

HAVE FUN WITH THE WALLS

If you eat in the kitchen, this part might not apply, since the decoration of the dining end will most likely have to coordinate with the rest of the room. But if you do have a separate space, this is where you can really have some fun. In a nutshell: you probably aren't in there very often, or for very long, so choose something dramatic and daring and something that you love but fear you would tire of if you looked at it for hours every day, in the sitting room or kitchen, for example.

This is the room for bold colours: dark shades always work in a dining room because you're usually in there in the evening. Candles will throw dramatic shadows up the dark walls and, unless you're Italian, you don't need to see too much. This is also where wallpaper comes into its own, and I'm not talking about a single feature wall. If you are going to go for it, you should go for it. Show it as the designer intended and wrap the room in it. Keep everything else quite simple and let the wallpaper speak for itself.

Some people can hang wallpaper themselves, but a professional can usually do a room in day which means that, cost of paper aside, it's a look you can change as often as budget and boredom will allow. In addition, if the wallpaper is providing the only colour and the window dressings are fairly plain and neutral, you can completely change the look of the room simply with a few rolls of paper. There are some new removable wallpapers coming to the market now, too. They have adhesive already on the back and you simply wet it to activate the glue. Some are in the form of very large murals, which can look stunning if you have the space. Others are plainer, which is brilliant if you live in a rental and aren't allowed to paint the walls. You can simply peel it off in one large sheet when you get bored or need to move on.

HANGING WALLPAPER: SOME GUIDELINES

First off, be aware that this may lead to divorce if you do it with a partner. We tried once and we finished shortly before we had to call the lawyers in, but it was a close-run thing. The paper was a mess – and that was before the then-two-year-old peeled away all the unstuck edges.

If it's your first time, a vinyl wallpaper is easier to handle as it's a bit more forgiving if you get it too wet or over-handle it. Alternatively, choose a paste-the-wall paper. It's much easier to manoeuvre dry paper onto a sticky wall and slide it into place than to wrestle with a long piece of wet, glue-filled paper that will inevitably try to wrap itself around you rather than the wall. This also means you don't need a trestle table to lay the paper on while you glue it.

Do get lots of samples and try to get one that's large enough to see the repeat. Failing that, a lot of companies now have visualisation tools, which means you can see what the whole wall will look like rather than just a small sample. This can make a difference if a pattern trails over the whole wall or just repeats in small designs that might look bitty when seen on large spaces. You do need to consider the overall effect when seen from a distance.

There's a design by the UK wallpaper company House of Mischief that looks at first glance like a conventional, if opulent, damask pattern. On closer inspection, the design is actually made up of couples indulging in what one can only politely describe as somewhat Kama Sutra. Granny almost certainly won't notice, but your neighbours are bound to. As will your boss.

Having said that, don't be afraid of big, bold patterns. This is not a room you live in, so you can afford to make brave choices; these will also stand out better in dim lighting. Wallpaper can hide lumpy, bumpy walls and save you paying a plasterer to do a skim. If this is a problem and you don't want patterned paper, consider the textured versions. Anaglypta only looks old-fashioned when it's painted in beige vinyl silk. Cover it in a flat matte contemporary grey or dark navy and it's a whole different, and more modern, ball game.

THE ALL-IMPORTANT STORAGE

One of the pieces of furniture I am most often asked to source is a sideboard for the kitchen or dining room. It's not always just about storage; a sideboard provides another surface for a lamp, or a plant, or even the television. If it's purely a dining room, you can put bottles of wine or dessert on it until they're needed. They're expensive pieces of furniture because there's a lot of work involved in making them; you'll just have to put some time in to hunting down the one you want, whether vintage or contemporary, upcycled or recycled.

Or course, not everyone wants a sideboard. Perhaps you prefer a vintage cupboard with a glass front so that you can see your collection of china. If that's the case, and your walls have been painted, think about covering the back of the cupboard with some wallpaper to add interest and so that it looks good even when empty. You can even use wrapping paper, if it's thick enough, rather than wallpaper. Or perhaps you have space for a dresser or some open shelves.

Whatever you use, it's a great way to house the overspill from the kitchen. Yep, I'm way ahead of you – this is where you were going to hide the juicer to bring it one step closer to the front door, and then the charity shop,

isn't it? The dining room is the one place where it's not just about storage for storage's sake. It's about finding a piece of furniture that looks good as well. Style *and* substance, if you will. If you have a dining room that has to double up as a home office (and we'll be dealing with that specifically in a later chapter), make sure you buy something that will happily store files and papers, and that the printer can slide in, or under, when not needed.

If you have a room that is called the dining room by the estate agent or landlord, but you don't need it for dining, decide on its purpose and decorate it to fit that. Don't just leave it as a space to keep the pram out of the hall, the filing that is waiting to be sorted and the laundry out of the kitchen. Don't waste space on spaces you don't need.

I've lost count of the number of dining rooms I've seen that are being used as enormous walk-in cupboards. As more of us opt for larger eat-in kitchens, we don't need a formal dining room. But instead of filling it with clutter, think about what you could use that space for. A playroom? A teenage hangout space? A really great home office or a spare bedroom for elderly relatives who can't get upstairs? Or maybe you really do need it to store lots of stuff, in which case build some good cupboards and storage units; don't just dump it all on the table and hope that the clutter fairy will drop by. She won't. She's in my loft.

Before we leave the dining room, there is one last piece of furniture that's perfect. In recent years it has become screamingly fashionable but, in my opinion, it will never go out of style. It is the drinks trolley, or bar cart as it is sometimes known. They tend to be small, so they can fit in an awkward alcove or corner and, of course, although they are a natural for the dining room they don't have to be in there. A glamorous brass and glass one will bring a Soho House vibe to your living room. An industrial metal one can store vegetables and live in the kitchen. You might even have room for one in the entrance hall, where it can hold plants and trinkets. It's a versatile bit of kit that you will always find a home for. I have one in my bathroom with smoked mirror shelves that holds towels and other bathroom stuff. It makes perfect decorative sense in a dining room, however, and will liven up an awkward little corner perfectly.

My grandmother had an antique wooden drinks trolley that was used to serve afternoon tea at 4.30pm sharp. My mother once expressed a slight thirst at 4pm and was brusquely told to wait. The tea was served from a brown china pot that had to be warmed first. Lapsang souchong, black, no sugar. My mother's second transgression was to once ask for a teabag in a mug. There was nearly fainting. At 5.30pm the trolley was wheeled away and its contents washed up so that my grandmother could be, as she liked to say, sat sitting for the BBC news at 6pm. This was followed by pink gins at 7pm when her favourite show, *The Archers*, came on Radio 4. It doesn't matter if you use your trolley for drinks or plants, books or bottles, you will always find a purpose for it. They're great in bathrooms for stuff. Kitchens for extra stuff. Halls for more of that stuff. You've got stuff; you probably need a trolley.

4

THE SITTING ROOM

The sitting room, the lounge, the drawing room or the reception. Whatever you choose to call it, this space should really be universally known by its other name: the living room. Sometimes we come in here just to sit, to play games or relax with a cup of tea. We might want to collapse in front of the telly after work or chat with friends over coffee or wine. It's a room that needs to suit myriad activities but it's also the one room of the house that needs to be completely comfortable to do nothing at all. To live, to breathe, or just simply to be.

This is a room you probably spend a lot of time in, so it's not the first place to start your experiments in. If you don't have a dining room in which to practise being daring, try the downstairs loo or the hall. Once you're comfortable mixing colours and adding patterns, bring your confidence to this room.

That's not to say it has to be boring, but you need to consider colours that work for you in every mood; not just when you're tired, but when you want to have a party too. This means you need to include something that makes your spirits soar, something that cheers you up after a rough day. This can be anything from a pattern on a rug that you never tire of seeing, to a cushion in a gorgeous colour or a vintage piece that brings back happy memories – and potentially all of those things.

Once again, you need to consider who uses the room when it comes to deciding on a colour scheme. Paint reacts differently in different lights, so before you choose a shade, make sure you've looked at it during the day and again at night when the lamps are lit. Then it's back to the honesty box. Do you come in here in the day? Or is it mainly the evening? Is it mostly used as a television room or is it a place to sit and talk? If you're fantasising about it being a place to sit and talk, but it's actually for Netflix and popcorn, then admit it.

I tend to go to my sitting room mostly at about 9pm, so it mainly needs to look good under electric light. It's painted dark grey – Down Pipe by Farrow & Ball – because that's a deep, rich colour that works during the day

continued >>>

THE SITTING ROOM *continued* >>>

but really comes alive at night. If you spend a lot of the daylight hours in your sitting room, you might want to choose something paler. That's not to say that you can't use opulent navy with gold accents, but you may find that you instinctively stay out of it during the day because it feels more like an evening space.

Try mixing it up a little so that it works for all scenarios. If you want the dark opulent colours but need to be in there in the day, consider using the half-painted wall trick from the hall chapter: deep, dark neutrals such as charcoal, navy or dark green on the bottom half with a lighter shade (or wallpaper?) above. Pale pink is very underrated as a warm neutral and looks fantastic when given a bit of edge with a charcoal sofa, which is a practical choice when it comes to mucky hands and sticky fingers. On the subject of pale pink, I know several women who have used this colour and shrieked: 'Pink? *Pink?* This is not pink, it's beige!' at their hapless husbands and partners. It is pink, by the way, but now it's called Millennial Pink and it's gender neutral, massively on trend and a fully macho colour – when teamed with black and gold.

You could also try something a little unexpected that works for both night and day. We once painted a chimney breast wall black and the fireplace neon pink, rather than the more traditional way round. It created instant wow factor at both ends of the day.

If your base is mainly monochrome or neutral, add colour with rugs and cushions that you can change with the seasons (which is code for when you get bored). Make sure there's something fun; I have a gold lamp in the shape of a palm tree. It's a little extreme, but it works for me. There is a real perception that because it's a house, you have to take it all incredibly seriously and only make sensible choices. No-one ever got excited by sensible choices. It is a house (or a flat) but it is above all else your home, with equal emphasis on both words. It's yours, so make it reflect who you are. And it's home, which is self-explanatory.

If you're starting from scratch, don't forget to go back to your wardrobe for colour inspiration. But having done that, don't assume that the strongest colour has to appear in the smallest amounts. If you love it, slap it all over the walls, or use it on the sofa instead of opting for that sensible, neutral goes-with-everything (whisper it: boring) shade. Dark walls and a teal or orange sofa will look fabulous. Throw in some monochrome patterned cushions and the space is starting to sing.

If colour isn't your thing, layer up the neutrals but make sure you bring in lots of different textures and materials to keep it interesting. Velvet and cashmere, linen and cotton can all be mixed up together and won't frighten the colour-phobes. Indeed, a restrained palette can look stunning, but if it's all in the same safe linen it might be a little boring.

One final tip: rather than relying on plain sofas and chairs and patterned cushions, reverse it. A single patterned armchair will look really confident and interesting in a sitting room and you can bring it down with a plain dark cushion. Don't assume the pattern has to go on the small stuff. Be brave – put it all over a chair.

Now you've got the rough idea, let's talk about rugs. There's so much choice out there, but choosing the size right is key to pulling the whole room together and showing it off to its best advantage.

This room doesn't have to multi-task, so much as work for many different moods. Are you relaxing with the family watching television or drinking wine with friends and chatting? It needs to be light in the daytime and cosy at night. Consider the colour scheme carefully and check it in both natural and electric light.

THE RULES
OF RUG LAYOUT

For every one person who says there's a rule, another will want to break it. For every one person who tells you to do it this way, another will disagree. So let me make it clear that these are just my rules; you may disagree, and you should feel free to experiment.

First up, and this is my personal number one: buy the biggest rug you can afford. It doesn't have to go all the way to the edge of the room – try leaving 45cm free around the edges – but aim either to have all the furniture on it, or at the very least, the front legs. Adapting that rule? Have the front legs of the sofa and chairs freestanding. What you want to avoid is a rug island in the middle of the room with all the furniture standing respectfully around the edge. A rug island with a coffee table marooned on top doesn't work either.

To start with, your visitors will feel that if the furniture isn't allowed on the rug then nor are they, which isn't a relaxing position from which to start the evening's entertainment. Secondly, the room looks disjointed. A large rug brings everything together and creates a unified space. This is absolutely key if you have a large open-plan space in which you have dining and sitting areas. Use rugs to zone the space.

Right, to the bedroom for rule two. If you have a large rug in the bedroom it needs to pretty much go under the whole bed with some sticking out at the end and both sides. You can keep the bedside tables off it if you like but don't, please, do that thing where you have a bit of rug the same width as the bed at the end. It looks terrible, as if you couldn't afford to buy a rug big enough for the room. If that was the case, and you couldn't, put that rug somewhere else.

Or use it for rule three. A bedside rug can float. You can have one on either side. These work particularly well if they're odd shapes. I use the boys' old sheepskins that they had in their prams by the sides of our bed.

Leaving the bedroom and going into the kitchen (or dining room) for rule four, you can absolutely have a rug under the table, but it must be large enough so that the chairs can be pulled out and remain on the rug. Otherwise, when people pull their chairs in the rug gets caught and rucks up underneath, and people trip. Especially if there is wine involved. Or, worse, coffee, which can be more staining. Again, if your rug ain't that big, put it somewhere else.

And finally, the exception to the rule: if it's an odd-shaped rug it can float like an island because it can lie at an angle, which therefore looks like you meant it. A small rectangular rug in the middle looks like you ran out of money, and that's absolutely not the effect we're aiming for here.

There is another idea if the space is big and the money is tight. Buy a piece of carpet and have the edges bound to turn it into a rug. Your local carpet fitter should know a place where you can have this done and it will work out much cheaper than buying a huge rug. We did this in the spare room with a large piece of grey carpet bound in neon pink to match the fireplace I mentioned earlier. It cost about a third of the price of a rug and, since it's a big room, was much more cost effective.

Now, for those of you that are left with a collection of small rugs that you can't use anywhere – there is a solution, and it's perfect for the sitting room where the coffee table can help to hold them in place: overlap them. I have four rugs in my sitting room for that very reason. They don't have to be the same pattern, but the colours should tone, or they can be the same design in different colours. Experiment. But, be aware, you are getting into rule-breaking territory so you need to be confident enough to trust your judgement here. One combination that always seems to work is that ubiquitous black-and-white stripy Rand rug from Ikea, which you can mix with vintage Persian, modern geometric and pretty flowers. It's big, it's cheap – it's from Ikea, so that's the point – it goes with everything and will bring a modern look and a healthy dose of black to the space (as discussed earlier, in the A Word About Colour).

It's like wearing a really outrageous outfit to a party – if you feel good in it, you'll look good. If you feel nervous, people can tell. The same with interior design. The basic, most important rule of them all is that *it has to look like you meant it.* If there's even the slightest hint of panic about what you've done, it will show.

GETTING THE LIGHTING RIGHT

We have already spoken about how important it is to have dimmer switches and lights on different circuits so you can change the mood, and the sitting room is one of the most important rooms for this. Sometimes you'll just need to flick on the overhead light when you come home from work and before you settle down for the evening. What is it with these TV thrillers where people are fumbling around in the dark for ages pouring drinks and getting undressed while the killer lurks unseen until it's too late? When I walk into a room the light goes on. No-one's going to be hiding behind my sofa for 20 minutes while I take my shoes off in the dark and put the music on.

So yes, a switch by the door for the pendant light. Then you need to think about the rest of the room, and you'll need different sources: floor, table, task and, sometimes, wall. These will all have different jobs – allowing you to read, watch television, thread that pesky sewing needle or chat quietly with friends and listen to music.

Now, if you don't have different circuits and don't want to spend a fortune retro-fitting, don't panic – you can cheat. We've put our lights on timers. This started as a security thing for when we were away on holiday, but has resulted in my becoming so

lazy that I am incapable of turning my own lights on and off, since everything happens automatically. Since we're talking about my house, I don't have a central pendant either. I tend to use my sitting room only in the evenings and I don't really need the brightness of an overhead light at that time of day; I want it a bit more atmospheric. And since the lamps are all on timers, I never walk into a dark room, so that burglar is going to have to rethink his strategy.

One of the other reasons I don't have a central light is that I don't have a ceiling rose in there. It was one of those things that was on the list to restore that simply hasn't happened yet. One of Sally's tips is that if you do have a ceiling rose and don't want a pendant lamp, you can hide a recessed spotlight in the middle of it and it will be almost completely invisible but will shine a soft beam of light down onto the coffee table below, highlighting your beautiful books, vase of flowers, half-drunk cup of coffee and tray of broken Lego models (tick as appropriate).

Sally also said that in one house she installed the secret spotlight, then hung a chandelier as well, which didn't give much light as it was mainly decorative, but the spotlight shone through it and reflected off all the crystal. Now, that's

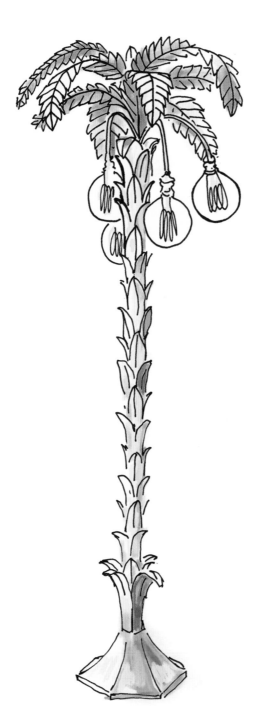

probably quite complicated to do, but if you've bought a vintage light that doesn't work, or a gorgeous chandelier that only works with candles, it might be something to consider.

Let's just have a final word about that pendant light. Yes, it might be functional, but there's a good chance that this is the one light in the house that really is there mostly for looks. It won't be on during the day and once you've located the burglar and thrown him out, you will probably be turning

continued >>>

GETTING THE LIGHTING RIGHT *continued* >>>

it off and putting on all the side lights for atmosphere. In other words, the ceiling light in this room is like the fabulous pair of earrings on the outfit, or the amazing necklace without which it's just a black dress. So don't just buy a boring paper shade and forget about it or if you do make sure it's massive – and I mean HUGE. Playing with scale is a really good trick to bring drama and confidence to a room. Alternatively, choose one that's sculptural and looks just as good off as on. If you want a plain drum shade, find one that's gold on the inside, which will look beautiful and also cast a very flattering light. In short, make sure it has earned its place in the room. You had to earn the money to pay for it, so it needs to pull its weight on the décor front. That's only reasonable and should apply to everything you buy.

The light in any room needs to come from above, the sides, and below if you are to create a truly layered scheme. Speaking of layering, another suggestion is picture lights. Now, before you start gasping in horror, these don't need to be those old-fashioned shiny brass things that belong in museums and at Granny's house. You can find very modern wall lights these days, and they can often be painted to match the wall, so they won't even show.

When it comes to table lights, you need a mixture here too. Make sure you have a task light that is bright enough to read, knit and generally see by. A general table light can be softer if it is just for atmosphere. A dark lampshade will send light up and down, whereas a pale one will diffuse it out softly all round. If you have shutters or curtains, you can install uplights below or downlights above to wash a gentle light over them in the evening. It's about playing with light and shadow and creating soft pools of light and interest.

Finally, if you have shelving, consider putting lights along the top to show off the books or objects you have on them. This could be in the form of another row of picture lights, for example; the lights themselves might not show that much, but the objects will. Or you could use the LED tape trick from the kitchen chapter (page 80).

SITTING ROOM LIGHTING: A CHECKLIST

☐ Always install a dimmer switch.

☐ Have your lights on different circuits so you can play with the atmosphere.

☐ Layer the lighting – with a mix of ceiling, wall, floor and table/task lamps.

☐ Vary the heights of your lights.

☐ Include a bright task light as well as softer table lights.

☐ Make the lighting work – is it showing off a fireplace, a vase, a row of books?

☐ Make sure the overhead light looks good when both on and off.

The sitting room is perhaps the room that most reflects your personality. Unlike the bathroom, bedroom and kitchen there is no fixed furniture here like a bed, a bath, an oven or a fridge so it's entirely up to you what you choose from the shape of the chairs to the colour and how many. More than any other it will house your collections of precious objects and possessions. This is the room where visitors and family get to see who you are. Whether you layer up colours and textures and ornaments in a form of exuberant maximalism or prefer a more understated quiet look, make sure your guests can find you in this space.

HANGING YOUR ARTWORK

This is one of the most commonly asked questions to all interior designers, and one of their most common complaints, too. It's not difficult to get right, once you know the rules, but it's very easy to get wrong. Put simply, the centre of the piece needs to be roughly at eye level for the person standing in front of it, give or take a few centimetres. And yes, I'm sure there are plenty of very tall people living with lots of very small people and the answer – as usual – lies somewhere in the middle.

If you've been hanging all your pictures much higher than this, they're going to seem scarily low to start with, but it does mean that you can actually look at the picture. Which I imagine is why you bought it in the first place, unless you liked it because it went with the cushions (we'll come to that in a minute). The same applies for a picture over a sofa, which will also make it quite low on the wall, but again means you can see it. This, incidentally, is why putting the television over the mantelpiece is always wrong. We're going to talk about the tech shortly, but anything over the mantelpiece is at eye level when you're standing in front of it – which means that when you're lying (sorry, sitting) on the sofa you'll give yourself a crick in the neck. And why would you want to do that?

If you're hanging one or two big pieces on a wall, try to ensure that the top of the picture isn't in a straight line with the top of the door. Move it up or down a little to avoid that, and the same goes if it's near a row of shelves. Try to have the top falling between two shelves to break up the lines.

So, that's the big picture – as it were – dealt with. Now what about the gallery wall? I get lots of emails from people panicking about how to do this. The true answer is that there are no rules, but I know that makes people nervous, so let's break it down into some simple guidelines and you can take it from there.

Firstly, you can put all shapes and sizes of image in a gallery wall, and all colours and styles too. Personally, I get a little nervous if there's too much going on, so if you're like me and have a wide variety of pictures, styles and colours, try framing them all the same way to bring some uniformity. A wall of black frames always looks good on a dark or light wall. Then, if you're feeling brave, you could throw in an antique gold or wooden one. But you can take it one step at a time, and that's the key to a gallery wall. If it's a collection of family pictures and postcards that you've gathered over time, it should look natural. Start with three or five, then build it around the edges so that it literally grows with your family.

When I was little I went through a phase of drawing giraffes – no, I don't know why – but look at the pattern of a giraffe. Its markings are irregular but they fit together loosely. You can have one large picture with a couple of small ones off to one side and another larger one above, overlapping the edges slightly to create a connection. That's the organic way to do it. But if it makes you nervous, the easiest thing to do – now that you've mastered Pinterest – is to search for an arrangement that pleases you and copy it.

Start by laying all your pictures on a table or the floor so that you can see if you have the right ones, and if you like the arrangement, then you can begin to fix them to the wall. One way to do this – for rentals and those nervous about banging a series of holes in the wall – is to use command strips, which are basically Velcro for walls. These will hold the picture in place and peel off if you want to move it or move out.

The final gallery wall is the real gallery wall. That is, a wall of same-size pictures, framed the same way and hung in rows or squares or rectangles, depending on the size of your wall. Looks stunning; nightmare to do. If that's your choice then, as before,

make sure the middle of the middle one is in the middle of your eyeline and start measuring. Command strips are perfect, as they'll fix the picture exactly where you want it. If you use picture cord it may stretch, and every picture has to have exactly the same length of cord; too many variables for the clean look that this requires.

If you're buying something from a local gallery or having something framed nearby it's worth seeing if they have a professional hanger who can come to your house. It's not just about them hanging it well, but about getting a fresh eye about where you want to hang something. They will also know how to get that elusive straight line.

A final word on artworks: you really shouldn't buy a piece to go with your cushions. Many people do, and it makes even the most expensive art look cheap. If anything, you should buy the piece you love and change the cushions if they clash, which they probably won't, as you will instinctively be drawn to a colour palette that works for you, so it will work in your house. If you don't fall in love with anything enough to buy it, then leave the wall blank, hang a mirror, paint it a dramatic colour that holds its own or bust out the wallpaper, which won't need any extra decoration from pictures.

BUYING A SOFA

Buying a new sofa is one of the larger purchases you will make for your home and you might think that choosing a colour that goes with the walls and carpet is all there is to it – but there are myriad key decisions that need to be made before you even begin to consider the fabric.

Richard Baker, who set up his traditional furniture-making business, Rume, 10 years ago in Hove, East Sussex, says: 'The sofa is the most important element of the room and you should always spend a little more money than you intended to get it right, then build the room around it. The colour is the last thing to consider because it is the one element that you can easily change.'

But when there are sofas available from £800 to £8,000 in a variety of shapes and configurations, where do you start?

First of all: size. Some people just want a sofa, settee, couch – call it what you will – that's long enough to take a nap on. Others would prefer two smaller pieces facing each other to create a more conversational vibe. Or perhaps you want an L-shaped or modular one to fit the whole family. And it's not just about how it fits in the room – you need to make sure it can get through your front door. Many

companies offer sofas with bolt on arms or legs that can be easily removed to help with this.

Try laying a newspaper template on the floor to help you choose the right size and give you a sense of how much room it's actually going to take up. Don't forget that wide arms mean less seating space, while a sofa with a high back may be more comfortable as it provides a head rest. However, this style will dominate in a room with lower ceilings. Low backs will give a sense of space and also emphasise the size of an open-plan room.

Crucially, you need to think really carefully about who will use your sofa: is it for entertaining guests or family downtime? If you want to lounge or watch TV, don't choose one where your knees will be lower than your hips. If you need more support, choose firmer foam or sprung back seats with high arms and legs; and if you want a deep sofa, make sure there are enough cushions to support your back. The key to that is the same as buying a mattress (which we'll come on to): when sitting on the sofa you shouldn't be able to slide your arm behind your back. If there's a big gap, you aren't getting enough support.

Once you've decided on the style, you need to consider the frame. Ideally you want a hardwood, such as beech, which makes a solid and durable frame. Softwoods, like pine, may warp and bend. However, many sofa frames are now made from chipboard, which may include a tiny element of hardwood, and this allows the manufacturer to claim it is a hardwood frame. Since this is going to be one of your more expensive purchases, don't be afraid to ask exactly what it's made from.

If you're buying from a store rather than online, trying lifting one front corner of the sofa: once you have lifted it 15cm high, the other front leg should have come off the ground too. If it hasn't, the frame is not rigid enough. The legs should be bolted in place, not just screwed, and the fixings should be attached with screws, glue and dowel pegs as well.

When it comes to the filling, it's a matter of personal preference. Feathers will need plumping up more often than foam, and they can clump together over time.

Once you're happy with all the above elements, *then* you can start to think about the fabric. These days, linen isn't necessarily the most practical choice. It tends to wear out easily and if a lot of your sitters wear jeans then the rivets will damage it in no time. Modern velvets often come with built-in stain guards (ask) and don't crush like they used to. Leather can be wiped clean and often improves with age.

Now, what colour do you fancy?

WHAT ABOUT
THE TECHNOLOGY?

This is the burning question. The one that everyone wants the perfect solution for. He wants to know how big a sound system he can get away with and she wants to know how to make the telly disappear. I'm sorry to stereotype, but I've yet to find it the other way round in any house I've been to.

There are several options. I'm not sure if any of them are perfect, but it's about what works for you in your house and what you can live with. The first point to note is that technology is getting smarter. The telly may be getting bigger, but for the most part it's getting flatter and thinner too, so it does at least take up less space. Sony has just released a speaker that looks like a lantern, and more and more people are buying projectors that they can aim at a blank wall when they need to, and which simply aren't there when they don't.

Mind you, we are coming full circle. I was watching a programme set in the 1960s the other day and noticed a television sitting inside a cabinet with a picture and a plant on top. 'What an utterly brilliant idea,' I thought to myself, before remembering that we all had those once upon a time and

we thought they were unutterably naff shortly after that time. It just goes to show that what goes around comes around. It also brings me back to my original point: the return of the television as furniture. This is relatively new at the time of writing, but where one leads the rest will follow. A couple of years ago, Samsung challenged the French design brothers Ronan and Erwan Bouroullec, to come up with something new for televisions on the basis that the flatness, blackness and thinness had to stop somewhere. They designed the Serif: television as furniture. It's wide enough to put something on top (not quite the bowl of fruit, but not far off) so that it becomes part of the room. It sits on elegant hairpin legs and comes in navy blue, white or burgundy. Even the back is covered in a fabric panel that slots on and off and hides the wires. Then Loewe came up with a flatscreen television surrounded by a brass mount with hollow brass legs to hide the cables. Both are ear-bleedingly expensive, but they're the first to reimagine the TV for the twenty-first century. The designer Yves Béhar, has come up with a television in a frame; you can select a picture to occupy the

continued >>>

WHAT ABOUT THE TECHNOLOGY *continued* >>>

screen when the TV itself is switched off. This works well if you want to try and hide it in a gallery wall, for example.

But for the rest of us who are still struggling with the traditional black box, what is the answer? First of all, do you even need it in the room? One client of mine had a television in the kitchen for the kids and one in the sitting room for family viewing. She didn't have a problem with it in the sitting room as that was partly the point, but she wanted to hide it in the kitchen. We looked at different walls, different heights and different solutions and you know what we came up with? Get rid of the telly. She realised that most of what she needed to see in there could be streamed on a laptop. The kids could watch a DVD on the computer and she could watch recipes and cooking programmes via the internet. So the television was removed completely.

Now, that won't work for everyone and we still have the sitting room to deal with. One obvious idea is to paint the wall dark behind it, which allows it to disappear somewhat and gives a slightly more cinematic effect when you're watching it. Painting the sitting room dark isn't for everyone, but there are variations: you could paint the wall dark halfway up, for example. It doesn't have to be black; you can look at dark green, navy blue or even brown as solutions. You can paint a dark vertical stripe on the wall that goes halfway behind the television. That looks as if you made a decorating decision and almost turns the television into a feature in its own right as it hangs across two colours.

If you have a large, flat wall, you can install a sliding screen that you can hide the TV behind, perhaps with a picture on it, and then slide across when you want to watch. I have seen that done to great effect in hotels and there's no reason why you can't do it in your own home. It works brilliantly if you have an alcove either side of the fireplace but no actual fireplace, so you have somewhere to slide the cover to. Alternatively, you can build a false wall over the front of the TV – since they are so slim these days it needn't take up much room.

Whatever you do, don't put it over the fireplace. As we discussed earlier, it's not a picture and that's too high for it; you'll end up with a bad neck. The screen should be in a straight line from your comfortable viewing eyeline (presumably seated) to the screen. On top of this, the mantelpiece is a great place for a fabulous piece of art or a mirror to bounce the light around. Don't stick a light-sucking black box in that precious space.

Once you've found somewhere to put it, the tricky question of all the wires raises its ugly head. What to do? Well, if you have the television on a sideboard you can keep all the boxes in there and drill holes in the back for the wires. Or you can create a false wall, which is what we have done. Our television sits on a shelf in the alcove to one side of the fireplace. The boxes all sit on the shelf below. At the back of the alcove we installed all the necessary sockets, then created a plywood board that slots in front of the plugs and behind the boxes and painted it the same colour as the wall. There are two finger holes at the side so it can be removed and it all looks tidy and wire-free because sadly it isn't, yet, wire-less.

So there are your options: make a feature of it as a piece of furniture, paint the wall to match it, hide the wires as much as you can and make the best of it. There are other solutions, such as hiding it in plain sight – in a gallery wall full of pictures, for example – but I always think that compromises both. You don't want to hang your beautiful pictures, which you have chosen and curated with love and care, in such a way that they have to go round a big black box. And you don't really want to be watching television with the distraction of a nude or landscape off to one side.

There's no perfect solution for this one: just what works best for you and your television-watching habits.

5

THE BEDROOM

The bedroom changes its function as we pass through life. It begins, as babies, as a place where we learn to be alone, to get ourselves to sleep and keep our own company. As toddlers and tweens it is a place to play and later, as teens, a space for study and screen. For many of us, it is the room where we will work and rest, relax and eat. Eventually it is just where we sleep again and we require nothing more of it than a comfy mattress and a place to hang our clothes.

But storage and sleeping aside, the colour of the bedroom is one of the most important colour decisions of the house. Dark for evening relaxation, or light and bright to get you up in the morning? Whether you're a lark or an owl, colour is crucial in this room.

Having said that, you don't have to have all four walls matching. Bear in mind that the bedhead, or wall behind the bed, will only show when you enter the room. You can be flamboyant there because you won't be looking at it while lying in bed reading or, come to think of it, sleeping. What is crucial is the wall at the end of the bed. If you have a window, the window dressings are important here. But if it's a wall, whether it's paper or paint, picture or portrait, it's going to be one of the first things you see when you open your eyes in the morning, so make sure it's something that makes you feel good.

Do not, on this occasion, follow my example. Years ago, when my husband worked in newspapers, he used to edit a column by the artist Tracey Emin. One year, as a thank you, she gave him a copy of her drawing of Kate Moss. Nude. This is what hangs on the wall at the end of our bed. It's not *completely* ideal to wake up to, I will say.

If you decide on a pale colour, try wrapping the whole room in it: skirting boards, radiators, doors and even the ceiling. This will not only blur the edges, which will make the space feel larger, but will also create a calming effect. You can absolutely do this with a dark colour too, but that's a braver choice, and while I can tell you it will look good, not everyone will feel comfortable with it. This all-over trick works for small rooms, too. If you break up a small space with white woodwork it can be quite distracting, as well as drawing your eye to the edges and the limitations of the space. Keep it all in one colour and it will look bigger.

Once you've painted the walls, you can add a really incredible headboard for a contrasting colour, or some gorgeous bed linen. It's up to you whether you do the whole cushion-on-the-bed thing. I have never quite understood it. It takes 20 minutes to fight your way through them to get into bed (and that's in addition to the ten minutes of moisturising we all seem to need these days; it's reaching the point where you have to go to bed earlier to fit it all in) and then you have to pick them all up off the floor in the morning. Also, who are they for? Once I'm dressed I leave the room until I go back up there to bed. Free yourself from cushion tyranny – buy a great bedspread and leave it at that.

WARDROBES AND CLOTHES STORAGE

Apart from sleeping, there's a good chance that the secondary function of your bedroom is clothes storage. Some of you will be lucky enough to have dressing rooms, but most of us are trying to cram a wardrobe into this space and still keep it zen and peaceful enough for sleeping.

Many of us seem to inherit fitted wardrobes. Most of us hate the doors they come with. I'm certainly not a fan of the wall-of-mirror look, which can make the place look like a gymnasium. Also the full-length view of self within seconds of waking up. No thank you. It's bad enough waking up to Kate Moss in the nude every day.

But if that's what you've got, and if you do I'm guessing you love all the storage it provides, if you hate the doors, change them. It's that simple. There are various hacks you can read about online, but the simple one is to get a local tradesman to fit new doors. They can be made from MDF (cheap) and painted or sprayed. Add some new handles and it's job done.

You could also use wallpaper here, either a mural to give you a 3D idea of a space you can float away to at night, or perhaps a *trompe l'oeil* effect. I don't mean nymphs cavorting around a fountain (although if that's your bag, who I am to argue?) but paper

that looks like upholstered leather or panelling. Alternatively, cover the doors in fabric. You can staple-gun it to a cheap wooden door and it will transform the look. If you're feeling really clever, insert a layer of foam to make it padded and more luxurious.

I'm not going to get involved in how you store your clothes (this isn't that book), but I will pass on a couple of good tips I've learned. One: use flat hangers, as they take up less space. When I transferred to wooden hangers I suddenly found my wardrobe was half empty, which was a mixed blessing as it just made more space for shopping.

It does lead me to the second point, however. If you're building a wardrobe from scratch, do make it big enough to allow for new clothes. You're not going to stop shopping, and we might all talk about throwing things out that we haven't worn for two years, or the old one-in-one-out policy, but I've met very few people who stick to it. I certainly don't.

If you are lucky enough to be starting from scratch and reconfiguring the whole space, perhaps to include an en suite, there is one key point you need to consider. Chances are you're considering making the biggest space the bedroom, the next biggest the bathroom and then seeing if you can

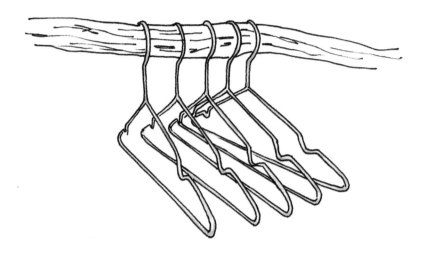

squeeze a dressing room or a walk-in wardrobe somewhere between the two.

Scrap that. The bedroom is mainly about the bed – the clue's in the name. If you're lucky enough to not need it for storage, you don't need it to be the biggest room. Arguably, it can be the smallest. A bed, a couple of bedside tables and reading lights and that's all you need. Where you will appreciate the space is the bathroom. A big bathroom is a luxury. It brings the hotel feeling to bedtime. And it's pretty good in the morning as well. So think about making the biggest space into the best bathroom you can afford, and perhaps the next biggest as storage: a walk-in or walk-through wardrobe that connects bedroom and bathroom. Or dividing a master bedroom into

dressing and bathing and putting the bed in the smaller space. Having lots of space to store clothes and get dressed will always feel like a luxury. So is a huge bedroom, but it can also be a waste of space.

We tackled this in a slightly different way in our house. There was a large master bedroom with a smaller bedroom next door. We turned the smaller bedroom into a bathroom and built a false wall in the big bedroom. This goes two-thirds of the way across and is about a third of the way from the back wall. Behind it is the wardrobe with hanging space and shelving up to the ceiling. The traditional Victorian alcoves on either side of the fireplace are used for shoe storage and the bed sits in front of this false wall, creating

continued >>>

a space with just it and two bedside tables. It is calm, uncluttered and, apart from Kate Moss, the perfect space to wake and sleep in.

Behind it is an unholy mess of clothes and bed linen. As I said, I'm not a declutterer but I know the theory. Now, whether this is possible will depend on how big you need the wardrobe to be but, taking the rules of clearance from the kitchen, you will need at least 1m at the end of the bed to walk comfortably around it. You will need at least 1m either side of the false wall for the same thing (we have 90cm and our wardrobe is slightly wider than the bed). You will also need approximately 60cm depth in the cupboard to allow for a standard hanger and we have 70cm to walk through – it's a corridor with clothes on one side, basically. You can play with these measurements to see what you can get away with. I have also added a little half door at the sides, which creates a boudoir effect, hides me getting dressed from the people in the house opposite and, in reality, means we can drape all those clothes over it that we can't be bothered to hang up at night. As a final touch, we had wiring put in so there are wall lights on the front by the bed and lamps behind on the shelves.

We have only one rail going all the way across and some high shelves. If I were doing it again I would have two rails and hang the few long dresses elsewhere, or at one end. That would double the storage at a stroke.

If we had stuck to the more traditional layout, we would have put wardrobes in the alcoves (which wouldn't have been large enough for all our clothes) and had a huge bedroom, possibly with an ottoman at the end of the bed and a chest of drawers. It's a look I love. But I know me, and I know him, and I know the cat. That ottoman would have been covered in clothes, both his and mine, and sprinkled with cat hairs, while the contents of the drawers would have been mostly on the floor or dumped on a chair. Those that did make it inside would be unlikely to have been folded and, therefore unlikely to be worn, frankly. Instead, we've created a space that looks completely tidy all the time because there are no surfaces for junk. And a large wardrobe behind the bed which holds everything else. Including that junk.

The first thing to decide in the bedroom is are you a lark or an owl? Do you want a cosy bedroom that is relaxing at night or something light and bright to help you get up in the morning? For a compromise, put a bold colour behind the bed so you see it when you walk in but not when you are lying down.

GETTING BEDROOM LIGHTING RIGHT

Given that we spend a third of our lives either sleeping, or attempting to do so, the lighting is just as important in this room as any other. And I have to admit, this is the one room where we haven't really paid quite as much attention as we should have done. So, to prevent you from making the same mistakes, here is my definitive guide to getting the lighting right in the bedroom.

First up, don't rule out overhead lighting. You may not use a central bulb much – we tend to use ours only to light the way to the switches by the bed. In this case, if you have a fitting there already, you could put a really decorative shade on it and make a feature. Or choose something really sculptural: like the pendant in the sitting room, it's mostly for decoration and this is one of the few places where you can legitimately embrace form over function.

Another trick is to change the fitting to a multi- or two-way outlet – that way you can have two flexes coming from the central bulb to two cup hooks on either side of the bed to create hanging bedside lights. This is a great space-saver and leaves more room on the bedside table for all those books that are on the 'to read' list (we all know what that means, but they still take up space while you're pretending you're

going to read them). If you do this, you should ask the electrician to add two more switches by the bed so you can turn them off without having to get out of bed.

Talking of switches, we opted for wall lights on the front of the wardrobe to save space and I spent ages lying on the bed trying to get them in the right place so I could just flick them off without moving. I failed. Now I spend every night stretching to the very tips of my fingers, failing, and wondering why I do this every day as I'm pretty sure I haven't grown since yesterday, before putting the book down, half-sitting and turning the light off. Every night. As first-world problems go, it's up there.

If your bedroom is the place where you dress and do make-up, Sally Storey suggests putting downlights around the edge of the room. This means they aren't shining in your face when you're in bed, but will provide good strong lighting for doing that make-up, or checking if both those socks are black or one is, in fact, navy blue. And we've all been *there* on a dark winter's morning.

Another of Sally's tips to add atmosphere is to consider a floor light. Make sure you have a pale shade so that the light diffuses out gently all over. A dark shade will create a pool of light above and below, which will be more dramatic and, perhaps, better in the sitting room.

BEDROOM LIGHTING: A CHECKLIST

☐ Make sure your lights are on different circuits.

☐ Install a dimmer switch.

☐ Don't be afraid of downlights in here.

☐ Bedside lights need easily accessible switches.

☐ You need versatile lighting for different tasks.

☐ Consider decorative pendant lighting.

CHOOSING
A MATTRESS

We all know the statistic that we spend a third of our lives asleep, but we probably also spend a third of our lives on the wrong mattress. I definitely have. I went to boarding school where the mattresses were made from horsehair and so bowed in the middle from generations of girls that there was very often only one sleeping position possible: on your back, in a straight line. Getting up in the morning meant you literally had to climb up and out. Then there were the years of student mattresses and cheap rented accommodation mattresses. Then, and this is the crucial one, there was the myth of the firm mattress.

When we uncovered this, in our forties, it was a revelation. Somewhere along the way, we seem to have been told that a firm mattress is what you want, that it's better for your back, your hips, your general well-being. So we always bought hard mattresses. Until one day my husband said that his back had been hurting for a while and it was time for a new mattress. My hips hurt when I lie on my side, I agreed. A trip was planned to the nearest department store in search of a new mattress.

And let's get this out of the way first of all – it wasn't cheap. But oh my, it IS wonderful. There are lots of mattresses

doing the rounds at the moment that come in a box and inflate and you can sleep on them for three months before you have to decide if you like it. All that is perfect, by all means try it out, but be aware of the following guidelines to see if it is actually the right one for you. We all know how to sit and stand properly but we seem to forget all about posture when we sleep. So we sleep badly. And we blame stress and wine and work. In fact the first thing to blame is the mattress. Get that right and some of the rest might sort itself out.

The first thing we discovered is that you need to be pretty heavy to sleep on a firm mattress. You need to be able to sink into it a little bit so that your spine remains straight. If you aren't heavy enough to sink, your spine will curve and your hip may hurt. It is possibly the first, and only, time in my life I have been too light for something. We moved around the store, lying on various hard mattresses and immediately saw the truth in this. So, like Goldilocks, we then lay on a few soft ones and immediately felt our backs bending and pressure on hips and lower backs. And then we found the medium one. The one that was just right. How did we know? Well, your shoulder and hip should sink in slightly so that your spine remains straight when you are lying on your side. You should then be able to slide your fingers – but not your whole hand – between your waist and the mattress. For anyone who does Pilates, your spine needs to be in the neutral position when you lie on your side.

Once you have found the right level of firmness, you can decide what you want your mattress to be made from, and that's a question of preference. A pocket-sprung mattress is made from individual springs that will prop up the whole body and, crucially, support each person and stop you rolling into each other in the middle of the night. Unless you want to, of course. A coil spring is the same principle but, as the name implies, one long coil. This will cost less but will still support you, although you may roll together more. The best bet is often a combination of springs and foam on the top layer to bring a hint of softness over the underlying strength. Or there's memory foam, which does as it says and conforms to your shape. Latex mattresses tend to be quite firm but very breathable so you won't overheat.

A mattress should last around 10 years if you turn it regularly to keep its shape. After that it will start to soften and reduce the support it gives you.

Now that you have an idea of what you're looking for, you're ready to go and try a few. Don't go when you're tired, as everything is bound to seem comfy then. Do lie on each one for a few minutes in different positions to see how it, and you, react.

CHOOSING
BEDSIDE TABLES

The bedside table is another hardworking piece of furniture and one that seems incredibly difficult to get right; there are an awful lot of ugly ones out there. For some reason manufacturers seem to think that if we are the type of person who wants a bedside table we must like the boxy, distressed, shabby-chic style of furniture. Every single client I have visited over the last six years has requested a good bedside table. I have come up with a variety of solutions and, I have to say up front, it's rarely one from the high street.

The first thing I always suggest is to go vintage. Old-school lockers and cupboards work well on either side of the bed if you like to store hand cream and tissues and all sorts of things like that. You can always paint them in a colour to suit if you don't like the original wood. If you can keep most of the things that clutter up the side of your bed in the bathroom and restrict it to a book, a phone charger and a lamp, then a simple stool often looks best, and forces you to be slightly disciplined about what goes there.

For many years we had the Kartell Componibili cupboards, which are sleek and modern and come in myriad colours. However, when I came to clear them out I found three compartments full of utter rubbish. I mean, there wasn't a single life-improving book in there, which might at least have justified the rest. No, it was old pens, notebooks, tissues – lots of those – lightbulbs, headache pills. You name it, it was there. And none of it needed to be there. It would all have been quite happy in the bathroom. Or the bin. So out it all went and in came two vintage Singer Sewing machine stools. The clock radio and my Kindle sit there happily. The notebook and pen on the floor by the bed. And that's it.

Another minimal solution is the bedside shelf. This frees up floor space and, as we shall see in the next chapter, the more floor you can see, the bigger the room appears. Paint the shelf to match the wall and it will disappear. Hell, you don't even need to stop at one shelf. Knock yourself out and have three. Just make sure that the tissues are in a pretty box and the shelves are far enough apart for a carafe of water and a glass to fit underneath as well. If space is tight at the sides of the bed, consider a long shelf running along the top of the bedhead. You can put a lamp at either end, a pile of books, water and everything else you might need. Because that's another thing: if you run out of horizontal space, go vertical. Use the walls, people, use the walls.

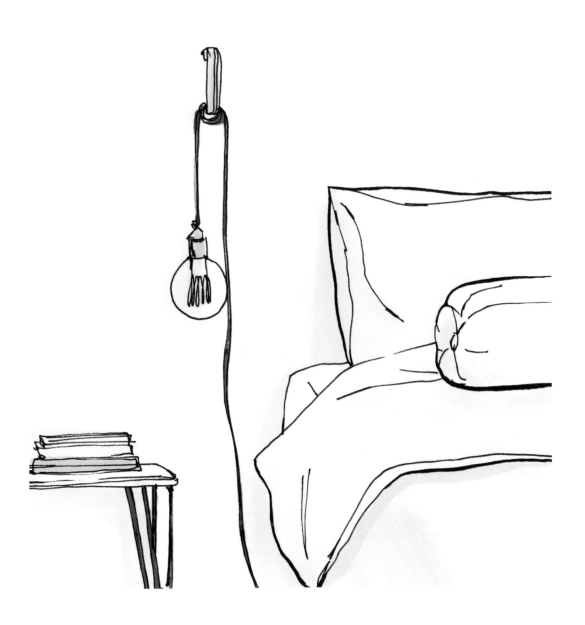

Décor is key to creating the right mood in the bedroom. One of the ways to do this is to keep the colours to a minimum. Painting the walls, skirting boards and door in the same shade is much more calming than breaking it up with white woodwork. In addition to that, arranging items in twos is also more soothing than odd numbers. Pairs are more calming as the eye isn't distracted by having too many different things to look at. If you have chosen a dark colour for your walls, use a mirror to bounce the light around.

6

THE
BATHROOM

Like the kitchen, the bathroom is a room that suffers from who we want to be rather than who we actually are. Everyone has a slightly different idea of what they want and that's before they've stopped to think about what they need.

Of course the primary function of the bathroom is cleanliness, but once we've all agreed on that, there's a whole raft of other stuff that starts to muddy the waters, as it were. Some want a relaxing haven where they can while away an hour in a cloud of scented bubbles, surrounded by flickering candles. Others want to get in, get clean, get out and get to work in the fastest, most efficient way possible. The problem comes when those two people live together. Throw in a couple of small children or, worse, two teenagers and this room, often one of the smallest in the house, has to be one of the hardest working. Once again, honesty is the key to happiness. You need to ask yourself some tough questions. Actually, it's not so much the questions as the answers. Planning the perfect bathroom requires both honesty and realism in equal measure. Now that the pep talk is out of the way and you're ready to face the truth, let's see what we can do about yours.

WHY THAT FREESTANDING TUB IS JUST AN EMPTY PROMISE

For those of you who are planning an imminent bathroom refurbishment, who hasn't got a picture of a fabulous freestanding bath, possibly in front of a fireplace, on one of their Pinterest boards? If you've been paying attention it will be on the fantasy board rather than the achievable board but, that aside, it's one of those classic bathroom dreams. Add a few candles – not in my case, as I'm a terrible catastrophist – some bubbles and a glass of something refreshing, preferably fizzing, and that's the dream right there.

But ask yourself this: how often do you actually have a bath? Of course some of you will be bath people and since you know who you are, you can skip this bit. For the rest of you: bathing? Do it often? For many of us, a freestanding bath is just a place to hang the towel on the way to the shower. It's a promise that come the weekend we will have time to sink into its luxurious depths for a precious hour of me-time without kids banging on the door, laundry piling up and deadlines pressing. I'm coming for you, bath, you think on a rainy Tuesday morning as you sprint past it to the shower. The promise of that bath can get you through the toughest of weeks. But come Saturday there's always something else to do, and once again the weekend slips by before you've had time to indulge.

If this is you, and if you don't have small children who still need to use the bath, then get rid of it. Buyers are much more flexible these days and they can always put the bath back in. Instead, think about using the space to install a massive walk-in shower. You can even have a seat in it. Now wouldn't you use that every day? And at weekends? And mightn't that be just as much of a luxury as a freestanding bath that doubles up as towel storage?

WHAT TO CONSIDER BEFORE
INSTALLING A SHOWER

Installing a shower might seem like a fairly straightforward thing to do, but if you're planning a bathroom refurbishment and thinking of changing from a shower over the bath to a walk-in, or considering removing the bath and putting in a large shower, there are a few points to consider.

It might seem obvious, but I find this helpful again and again (particularly with kitchens and bathrooms, which are the two most expensive rooms to decorate): you need to really think about who is using this room and how they use it. Do you have teenage bathroom hoggers? Do you have small children, in which case losing the bath is not an option? Do you have elderly parents visiting who would find a walk-in shower easier than climbing over the side of a bath? Think about it and be honest.

You might fancy the idea of a huge overhead shower (hotel bathrooms are another common fantasy) but remember that they are harder to clean as they don't come off the wall. This also means it's harder to clean the shower walls. If that is what you want, think about having a hand-held attachment as well.

Now for some technical advice I was given by the designers at Ripples, the London-based bathroom design company. First up, think about your water pressure. This is one for the plumber, but, there's no point spending hundreds of pounds on a massive rainfall shower head the size of a dinner plate if the water pressure is rubbish. Do you need to install a pump? If this is a second bathroom or en suite, will your boiler stand up to providing two hot showers at once?

Is this your forever house? In which case, do you need to think about non-slip tiles? They're much more stylish than they used to be. Is it worth putting a seat into the shower? Again, walk-in showers are better for older people as it can be tricky to climb over the edge of a bath. Always install the biggest shower cubicle you can fit in the space. Glass doors can be custom-made so you don't need to worry about that. Bigger is better: it's more luxurious, it's more hotel. It's just more.

If you're having a walk-in shower, make sure you can keep the towels within reach, but not so close they get wet. It's the same with the loo seat and anything you keep by the basin. It's better not to have a step into the shower if at all possible. This is true for all ages. The more flush with the floor the better, as this makes it easier to clean – you'd be amazed how scummy soap residue becomes, and it's a nightmare to clean all the tiny nooks and crannies in a shower – and if it's low it's less of a trip hazard. So, if possible, go for a flush fitting that can be set into a tiled floor on a slight gradient to allow the water to drain, or a very shallow tray.

Can you afford not to have underfloor heating? When we refitted our shower room, the builder suggested we install it. We weren't having a shower tray but were installing a drain in the tiled floor. It's a tiny room and the underfloor heating wouldn't have cost that much. We didn't do it because we didn't dare spend any more money and, we figured, it's not a very cold room so the heated towel rail would be sufficient. Well, here's the thing: underfloor heating dries the water up more quickly and stops it sitting on the floor, making limescale stains and being slippery. We should have, but we didn't. Coulda, woulda, shoulda.

When it comes to bathroom storage, you always need more than you think. It's like sockets in the kitchen. You might think you're going to exist in a minimalist haven of beautifully packaged bottles and jars, but you aren't. At some point that giant bargain-size bottle of shampoo just isn't going to be decanted, and you have to put that huge bag of cotton wool balls somewhere. Think about installing a niche in the shower for the things you need every day; you can add LED lighting strips to make a really good feature of it. Make sure you have ample cupboards or shelves built elsewhere – you will need them.

Finally, talking of lighting, don't assume it has to be downlights. Do you want a dimmer? That's a rhetorical question – have you even read the last few chapters? Do you want the light to come on automatically in the shower? Do you want a chandelier? There are lots of options. Some years ago we were staying in a hotel with a shower that had different coloured lights that changed in rotation as well as a radio that came on automatically when you turned the water on. Our younger son, who was then about seven, called it the Disco Shower and it was very hard to get him out of it. He still talks about it eight years later. And, frankly, he's never been as clean since.

Two basins are said to be the key to a happy marriage and it is, after all, one less row to have in the morning. This is my bathroom with very clearly defined his and her sides. The vintage counter is a way of softening all the hard white lines that you find in a bathroom.

HOW TO **PLAN** THE
PERFECT BATHROOM

Now that you've decided if you're Team Bath or Team Shower and worked out how much of a shower you can install, it's time to look at the rest of the room. First up, basins. If you have space for two, buy two. Some say it's the secret to a happy marriage, and I can see that. After all, there's enough to do in the morning without elbowing each other out of the way as you try to clean your teeth and do your mascara while someone else is trying to wash their face and do their hair. So two basins good. Failing that, like the shower, buy the widest one you can, so that there's at least a chance of two people using it together without a fight.

You will need some storage under the basin(s), so think about whether you want a modern vanity unit or an old vintage table and mount the basin on that. A final word on basins and a thought about the loo. It's an old trick, but one that works – the more floor space you can see the bigger the room will look. So, wall-mounted basins and loos are a good idea in smaller rooms.

Now there's one more area where you need to be brutally honest with yourself and that's storage. Those pretty glass bottles from the French flea market are more decorative than useful, which means you need storage for the stuff you use and a shelf for the pretties. Equally, you're going to keep collecting free samples from magazines that you bought just for the sample but will neither use nor throw away. You have more stuff than you think; you need more storage than you think.

If you have a wall-mounted loo with a hidden or built-in cistern, consider putting shelves over it up to the ceiling, perhaps adding a door to turn it into a cupboard. You can buy wall-mounted vanity units (don't forget the floor space) as well as mirror cabinets that you can sink into the wall above the basin so they don't stick out into the room, taking up more valuable space.

Finally, the decoration. It's the most important but also the least important element of the bathroom, partly because it's the most changeable, whereas you're going to be living with the other stuff for a while so you need to get it right. Mirrors are necessary but also key to bouncing light around – a godsend in a small, or dark, bathroom. If you have space for a small vintage stool, that will always look great. Wood will soften all those clean white lines and hard surfaces. And it's handy for resting a glass of wine or a towel on while you're luxuriating under that enormous shower.

There are so many magnificent tiles around at the moment that there's no excuse for not having some fun and bringing some personality into the room. You can use patterned tiles as a splashback for the basin(s), but think also about taking them from floor to ceiling in a stripe, or laying them in a rug shape around the bath. If you prefer plain metro tiles, consider laying them in a herringbone rather than the traditional brick pattern.

I have installed a wall of foxed mirror tiles in my bathroom, rather than modern glass. This fits well with the modern rustic feel of the room and, as I mentioned earlier, stops the room looking as though you're about to start exercising in there. Although, if you are, don't let me stop you.

Now that you've worked out who the bathroom is for, what they are going to be doing in there and how long it is going to take them, you can start planning the perfect space. Then, and only then, can you start shopping.

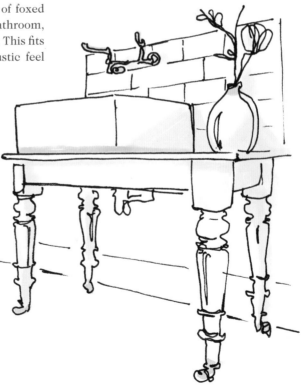

GETTING **BATHROOM LIGHTING** RIGHT

I expect most of us just have a row, square or rectangle of downlights that may or may not be on a dimmer switch. If yours are, score an extra point and pass directly to the Spare Room, collecting your £200 on the way. The rest of you need to read this.

As you will remember from earlier chapters, I invited the creative director of John Cullen Lighting, Sally Storey, to come to my house and point out where I had gone wrong (quite often) and what I could improve (quite a lot).

When we did our bathroom, in the far-off days before Pinterest, I had cut out a picture of a large freestanding bath with a chandelier over the top and stuck it to my real-life moodboard (I know, quaint, isn't it?). 'No,' said the builder when he saw it. 'You can't have that. Regulations is regulations and you can't have that.' I didn't get the chandelier, and I've been standing under a spotlight grid for the last five years. Not only that, most of them aren't in the right place either. I think it was more about the builder not being sure of the regulations and, more to the point, not being bothered to find out, because you can have a chandelier within certain parameters. Read on…

The first thing you need to know when tackling bathroom lighting is that the room is zoned according to the distance between the water and the light fitting. So Zone 0 is basically in the bath and on the floor of the shower – the really wet bit. Zone 1 is within the shower enclosure or directly behind the bath – high chance of getting really quite wet. Zone 2 stretches for 60cm around the outside of the shower and the ends of the bath (see Zone 1, if you have small children). If you want a chandelier over the bath it needs to be 1.5m from the top of the water when the bath is filled; in other words, you need a ceiling around 2.25m high. This rules out a pendant over the bath for most of us, but you might be able to have one in Zone 2, so that it's not over the water – the middle of the room, for example, if the bath is to one side.

All is not lost if you can't have a statement pendant in your bathroom. Consider wall lights, which will reflect onto the water in the bath and create a gorgeous, shimmering effect that will be really atmospheric. Or you can stick a downlight over the shower to highlight your tiles. Wall lights on either side of the mirror will give you enough illumination to shave and apply make-up and will create a soft, ambient glow for that bath you promised to have.

Many of us with bathrooms in loft conversions will have awkward sloping ceilings to contend with. Instead of putting spots in the ceiling at an angle, put lights on the wall to wash light gently down, or use floor lights to highlight the basin or bath. Then, when you've sorted out which lights you want and where to put them, you need fittings with the correct IP rating. Are you beginning to see why most of us just fit spotlights and go to the pub?

Basically, if it's directly over a bath or shower (Zone 0) it needs an IP rating of 44. (You should always check technical details with your builder, but understanding the parameters can be useful when you're trying to find the right thing.) IP is to do with the distance between the electricity and the chances of splashing or immersion, which are filed under Things To Be Avoided.

It's probably easier to get the builder to deal with the technical side, but don't take the first no for an answer. And do consider making lighting an integral part of the bathroom to create a bright, well-lit space in the morning and something a bit more atmospheric with rippling water patterns shimmering on the walls in the evening.

BATHROOM LIGHTING: A CHECKLIST

☐ Fit a dimmer.

☐ Don't make downlights the only source of light in the bathroom.

☐ If you have a niche, light it with LED strips.

☐ Use wall lights by the mirror and in alcoves.

☐ Consider a statement pendant (in the correct zone) if you have the ceiling height available.

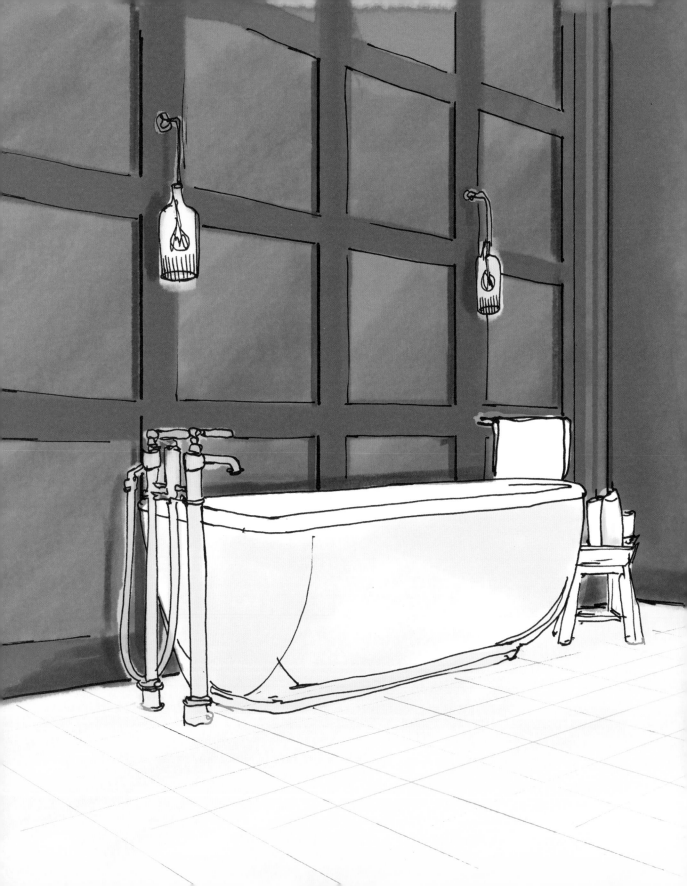

7

THE
SPARE
ROOM

The spare room or home office is another really busy room that often has to multi-task, but this chapter will show you how to make it all work. These days, having a spare room is a real luxury. Even the name implies that it isn't really needed. But that's the irony; we could all do with a spare room, one that can do all the jobs that are overflowing from the rest of the house: store the drying laundry and the clean linen; give the teenagers somewhere to go to play their screens so you can watch television; provide a quiet corner for you to work in and a place for guests to sleep. This room, which is usually the smallest, often has to do all those things, sometimes all on the same day. This is a room where you have to think clever.

Spare room has come to mean guest room, but how often do we really have guests? Perhaps, if you added up all the guest nights, it's a month or two? That leaves 10 months of the year when this room is unused. So why have you put your old double bed in it – isn't that just a gigantic waste of space? Does it double up as a home office? All the time or just when you're 'working from home' and need something a little more substantial than the laptop on the sofa? This room is as busy as you, so its décor should probably be calm to help you remain calm, too.

The way to do that is opt for pale, cool colours such as soft greys, warmed up with natural wood. Arrange things with care on the shelves or mantelpiece. Hang some art. Make sure there's lots of lighting that works for every scenario – reading in bed, watching screens, working at the desk.

Every piece of furniture has to earn its keep by doing at least two jobs – so it's a sofa and a bed, a dressing table and a desk, a stool and a bedside table, a desk chair and a place to drape your dressing gown. A cupboard to store the sheets and hide the printer.

You are trying to create a room that can function as an office all day and then, with a quick flip of this, shove of that, swivel of the other and a bunch

continued >>>

THE SPARE ROOM *continued* >>>

of flowers, it's a guest room. It's the same principle if you work in the dining room, by the way. If you have a sideboard, make sure it can store your work stuff as well as spare serving dishes. Instead of bookshelves filled

with box files perhaps you could put a door on the front to hide them when the room is used for its designated purpose.

But back to the spare room. First things first: the sofa bed. While many of the same rules apply to sofa beds as to choosing a sofa, you do need to be realistic about whether your first requirement is a sofa with occasional sleeping, in which case a foam mattress will be fine, or if the quality of the bed is paramount, which if it's for parents and grandparents might be the case. A pocket-sprung mattress is more expensive but it can be used more frequently and provides better back support. So you need to read the chapters on buying a sofa and buying a mattress, then look at your bank account and decide accordingly.

Sadly, the sofa bed market is largely lacking in style. In the middle of the market there are a lot of very conventional sofas out there, so you'll need to spend more if you want something a little more design-led. We opted for an L-shape as it fitted into the room better and meant it could fit more teenagers on it. I was quite keen on two singles facing each other as I thought that would look better but for some reason my mother-in-law didn't seem to think that was a good idea for her and my father-in-law. Nor, in fact, did my mother, who comes on her own. So that idea went out of the window, then. Mind you, the only sofa bed to which I was prepared to give house room folded out sideways, perhaps because it was an L-shape, which means that when it's a bed, someone has to climb over the back to get to the loo in the middle of the night. Funnily enough, the in-laws didn't fancy that, either. Guess who sleeps on the sofa bed when we have guests?

It's definitely worth trying to find a sofa bed with storage, as you need to find somewhere to keep the pillows and bedding when not in use. Often it's the L-shape ones that have that. Or invest in those storage bags that you can suck the air out of to compress everything into tiny boxes and shove them underneath if there's space.

I also keep a little bag of samples under my sofa bed – all those mini shampoos and handcreams, a couple of toothpastes and a spare deodorant, often the small ones left over from holidays. Sometimes, very occasionally (really, almost never), it's the one from a hotel that fell into my bag when I was packing at the end of the holiday. You can lay them out in a bowl for guests

and it makes it all feel a little more boutique hotel and luxurious. Which, if you're expecting them to sleep among your filing cabinet and paperwork, might go some way to alleviate the idea that they're just camping in your office for a couple of nights.

The next key bit of furniture is the desk. Ideally, this will double up as a dressing table. If the room is small, a narrow console table can work brilliantly here, especially if you work on a laptop. You can add a task light or even – using the long flex trick from earlier in the book – have a pendant light hanging to one side of the desk, which will free up even more space. As ever, storage is important here. Consider running a narrow shelf – or two – all the way round the room. You can store files on these and if you buy pretty ones that coordinate with the décor, that will look fine when it's a bedroom. You can also add books for guests and even pictures propped up on it as décor. If there's no room for a wardrobe then you can add wooden Shaker pegs all the way round under the shelves. Put a few hangers there and it's a guest wardrobe already.

When it comes to the décor you need to decide if you're using it more

continued >>>

THE SPARE ROOM *continued* >>>

often as bedroom or an office, although either way, there's no reason you can't have a little fun in here. These days, you don't have to paint the whole wall – you can, as we discussed earlier, paint half of it. Or you can paint a massive stripe, in front of which you can put the desk-cum-dressing table. Or a triangle over one corner to create a sitting area and zone it. The interior designer Daniel Hopwood painted a series of geometric shapes on one wall of a project he was working on but (and here's the clever bit) he did a pale blush as the background and the shapes in a darker version of the same colour so that it wasn't too full-on in either sleeping or working mode. You can, of course, be as bold as you like. I have a series of triangles painted on my spare room wall in shades of grey and pink.

A couple of other things that are worth considering for this room. If it's mainly used by parents coming to stay, an armchair and a television are a good idea if you can squeeze them in. Sometimes they need a break from hordes of rampaging toddlers and a 20-minute pause with a gin and tonic and the news, away from the rest of the family, can work wonders for everyone. I was talking about parents, but if they're offering to do tea, bath

and bed while you sit in the spare room with the gin, then you'll be glad you were able to do it in comfort. The television can be small and fixed to the wall so it takes up less space.

So far we've looked at the spare room from the sleeping/working perspective, but if you work from home for any length of time you need to think about whether it's actually the place you want to be. As I said earlier, it's usually the smallest room in the house. It's often at the top of the house. Or the box room. Do you really want to spend several hours every day in there? In our last house the spare room was at the top of three flights of stairs and under the eaves. It was small and airless with a tiny window and a sloping roof on which I hit my head with monotonous regularity every time I stood up. Things came to a (painful) head one afternoon when I had to write a newspaper feature on deadline. We didn't have a stairgate and my younger son, then aged about two, wasn't at nursery that day. I parked him in the sitting room surrounded by toys and sprinted to the top floor, wrote a couple of paragraphs, jumped up, hit my head, sprinted back downstairs, took the fake coal from the fake fireplace out of his mouth and legged it back up again. Two more sentences, one more head bang, and then back down. I know this doesn't make sense. Yes, I should have brought him upstairs with me, but he would have wanted to sit on my lap, or chew the computer cable or start trying to open the door and roll headfirst down the stairs because we didn't have that stairgate. Somehow, it seemed the least worst option. Anyway, that was the last time I worked in the spare room. For the next five years I worked at the kitchen table. This made sense: it was the nicest room in the house with the best view of the garden, and it was closer to the children. The other moral of this story is: buy a stairgate. Or a playpen. You can sit in it and they won't be able to mess with the keys on your computer.

Having said that, working in the so-called public areas of the house means you need to get very clever with storage because you have to clear up at the end of every day. It's like keeping an office in a box that you can wrap and unwrap in a matter of minutes. One way to tackle this is the 'office in a cupboard'. You don't have to sit there all day, but it will store all your paperwork, the printer and so on. It works thus: If you have an alcove, fit it with shelves, making sure the lowest shelf is high

enough to slide a stool (or chair, if it's a deep alcove) underneath, operating as a compact desk space. Fill the rest of the shelves with everything you need, add electricity for the printer, the computer charger and a desk lamp, and away you go. Fit a couple of doors – two half-width doors will take up less space when open than one standard-size door – and there's your office in a cupboard. This arrangement works in a sitting room so you can shut the door on it at the end of the day, and also in a bedroom, or even a kitchen. My very first home office was in the wardrobe. I used to shove the clothes along the rail to one side to reveal the computer nestling beneath. You could perhaps remove the clothes altogether, which might make for a more productive environment.

The other key element to working from home is that it really does have to be a space that calls you in. A space that you want to be in, otherwise what's the point? So in addition to arranging it how you want and how you like to work, you need to fill it with things you love. Add pictures on the walls, a comfy chair and paint it in a colour you love. If it's in a cupboard you're going to shut the door on it at night so

continued >>>

THE SPARE ROOM *continued >>>*

it doesn't matter if it's a vibrant colour that doesn't quite fit with the rest of the room, as long as it inspires you during the working day.

Finally, you probably have shelves in every room, and these days they're not just a place to store things. I am often asked for help in styling mantelpieces and windowsills as well as bookshelves,

so here are some guidelines to get you started. Arranging your office shelves with a mix of work stuff and treasures will make you happier to be in there, after all.

STYLING THE PERFECT SHELFIE

☐ HEIGHT: make sure there is variation. Books upright, books on their sides. A tall candlestick and a short one on the pile of books. Let the eye travel along.

☐ LAYER: unless your shelf is very narrow, try not to have everything in a straight line. Put the candlestick in front of the postcard that's propped up at the back. Let the necklaces hang down from the jewellery stand and pool on the book below.

☐ ODD NUMBERS: generally speaking, things group better in threes or fives. If you can mix the height within the group, you're already halfway there. But that's not to say you can't go for symmetrical – a candle at each end, for example. But then bring in some odd numbers.

☐ RANDOM STUFF: of course you want to display your bottles of scent and your family photos, but this is also the perfect place for that fabulous stone you brought back from the beach last summer, or that shell that you haven't been quite sure what to do with. This is the spot for the random treasures that don't quite make sense on their own but which mean something to you. But don't just buy something for the sake of it; this shelfie, as much as the rest of your house, should tell your story. It's about your treasures or bathroom necessities. It's not just for Instagram, you know.

☐ DON'T BE AFRAID OF THE EMPTY SPACE: designers call this negative space, but it basically means don't cram it all in. Give your things room to breathe.

☐ AND FINALLY: if in doubt, a little posy of flowers or a plant will often bring your shelfie to life.

Another hard-working room and a misnomer as it's usually the opposite of "spare". This room has to house guests, offices, drying laundry, teenagers and their screens and possibly even the odd bicycle. Multi-tasking furniture is your friend – the sofa bed, the desk that can double as a dressing table, the extra stool that can sit by the bed for a lamp and a book. Try to make sure that every piece of furniture in this room has at least one job and is capable of two. That is the key to success here.

MY
TOP 10
DESIGN
HACKS

This chapter is for the tweaks: the 10 things you can do to every single room that will instantly improve it. It's for those of you who aren't planning a major refurbishment, or who don't want to call in the decorators because you rent or because you have other things to think about right now. Follow these 10 steps in every room and you will have improved it. It's that simple.

1

SOMETHING NEW, SOMETHING OLD, SOMETHING BLACK, SOMETHING GOLD

This little mantra came about after I realised that it's something I tend to do in every room by instinct, and it really works.

Something new: There's always something new, just make sure it isn't everything. In my sitting room it was the sofa. It might be the curtains, or the table, or the lamp you found in that cute furniture shop on holiday. That's not to say I wouldn't have a vintage sofa and reupholster it, because I totally would. I've actually got my eye on my mother's, which came, in turn, from her grandmother's house, but it would appear that my mother hasn't finished with it yet, so I've had to buy something new in the meantime.

Something old: I see so many people who start again when they move house, but it's really important to keep things that have travelled with you through your life. Whether it's an old chair from Granny's house, or even an old chair from someone else's granny's house, a vintage piece will bring character to a room. It doesn't have to be furniture, but can be objects for the mantelpiece, pictures or books, an old wooden stool. Actually, this rhyme cheats a little because it doesn't include wood. Every room needs some natural wood, preferably old, so add a vintage wooden bench and you've killed those two birds. I have something vintage in every single room, from the coffee table I found in a junk shop (back in the days when such places existed and didn't all call themselves antique shops) to the bedroom table I found by the side of the road on my way back from the tip (the irony). The rugs are all old: some of them I have managed to relieve my mother of, some we bought. Probably we'd prefer one huge one, which would be less of a trip hazard, but they are always fiendishly expensive so we've layered them up (for more advice on the rules of rugs see page 110).

Something black: a drop of black will anchor the space and bring definition, otherwise it can all end up looking a bit wishy-washy. So whether it's the legs on the old stool, a collection of picture frames or a strong pattern on a cushion, always try to include a little bit of black somewhere in the room. If you favour lots of pastel colours and a more summery vibe, lighten the black to charcoal. It will be a little less heavy, but adding it will bring definition to the room and finish it off perfectly.

Something gold: it doesn't have to be gold, but that makes it easier to remember. It does have to be metallic, however, and that can be anything from a mirror to bounce the light around, to a gold pineapple ice bucket (or my 6ft brass lamp in the shape of a palm tree).

2 TIME TO GO GREEN

This is a recent addition to the top 10, but it's a fad that has become a trend and is actually, like grey paint, here to stay for the foreseeable future, so it deserves a place in the list. Yes, it's time to go green, and I don't mean put the recycling out. This time it's all about plants.

Before you panic, it's not about those dusty old cheese plants you had as a student, but about creating pockets of green loveliness in your home. I don't really understand why plants went out of fashion – after all, flowers never did – but ours is not to reason why, and the thing is that they are *back*.

Suddenly, every room looks better with a plant in it. Now, my husband is not terribly keen on plants, and has been giving the fiddle-leaf fig in the kitchen the side-eye for some months now (it doesn't care, it's growing like a weed and taking up even more space. It is definitely winning the battle of the side-eye). But when we had finished decorating the bathroom we were standing about arranging bottles of shampoo and stuff – as you do when you have a new room to play with – and he suddenly said: 'Do you know what this room needs?' 'What?' I said, expecting some sort of magazine-rack-type scenario (I mean, I know everyone reads in the bathroom but I'm not sure we want to advertise the fact, do we?) But that is not what he said. 'A plant,' he said. 'Yer wot?' I said, elegantly, for my gob was somewhat smacked.

We were out of that bathroom and down to the garden centre quicker than it was probably legal to drive; I had to get him there before he changed his mind. We came back with a large palm-like thing. I have no idea what it is but it definitely, definitely finishes off the space perfectly – even he says so. Of course there's no side-eye for this one, as it was his idea.

You don't have to have real plants, and I will own up to a 50 per cent kill rate with mine. It's screamingly fashionable to go fake these days – or, as we must now call it, *faux*, darling, *faux*. The key to using these is to mix them in with the real ones. Ideally put a real one at the front, then layer up with some faux at the back. That way if anyone touches a leaf it will be a real one and they will assume the rest are. Unless it's next to a radiator, which might give your game away, not that it really matters.

The other point is to choose your faux plants carefully. A cheese plant will always be easier to fake than a fern because the leaves are pretty plasticky

to begin with. It is, however, a truth universally acknowledged that you get what you pay for. Some of the best fake plants cost a lot of money. It's not out of the way to spend around £100 on a fake cactus for example. So if you've found one for £20 online, don't expect miracles, and if it's too much of a faff to return it, hide it at the back.

It seems to be another universal truth that all fake plants come in rubbish fake pots. They are always too small and instantly give the game away. If you're serious about faking it, you'll need to invest in new pots as well. They don't have to be expensive – my fake *Monstera* (cheese plant) now sits in a rather snazzy wooden bin that cost a tenner.

3 REMEMBER THE TOUCH POINTS

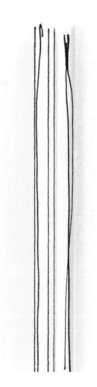

Like me, you've probably read about how supermarkets spend thousands of pounds researching how to arrange their shelves. They want the hard-to-sell stuff at eye level so that you see it first, and they'll make you bend down for the things they know you will buy anyway because they're the necessities. It's broadly similar in your home. The eye-level and touch points – light switches and door handles – are crucially important, yet are so often the things we don't even bother about.

I have changed all my light switches to black ones with a dolly toggle. They look so much nicer than the generic white plastic and even though the white plastic ones disappeared into the wall, I prefer these. We decided to make a feature of them and, I have to tell you, the children find the dolly toggle so satisfying that I swear they're remembering to turn lights off more.

In the same vein, I have leather handles on my kitchen cupboards. They're great to touch and soften all the hard lines of the kitchen, which is full of stainless steel and straight lines. Another trick is to paint the inside of your cupboards in a colour that makes your spirit soar like a hawk every time you see it. It's very subtle, as it's not on view all the time, so you can afford to be daring: metallic gold, neon pink, or a beautiful, calming and restful green. Pick a colour you love and it's a little visual treat every time you reach for the biscuit tin – and so much less calorific. It's a small thing, but it will make a big

difference to your experience of using your home, which is, after all, as Le Corbusier said: 'a machine for living in'. Another simple change is electric flex. This isn't, strictly speaking, a touch point, but it will make a big difference. I have changed all the plastic cords on my pendant lights to fabric. It costs less than a fiver a metre and it makes a real difference. There are dozens of colours available, so you can make a statement with bright pink or red (and I have done both of those) or keep it simple with black. I've done that too. It's even cheaper if you know how to wire it yourself, which I, sadly, don't.

Another trick is to paint the edge of the door in the same colour as the room – if the door is white. This just gives a hint of colour and only shows when the door is open. It's a tiny detail, but one that counts.

4 LAYER THOSE LIGHTS

I've written about lighting in detail for each room in earlier chapters, but to summarise:

One overhead pendant is not enough lighting. If it's all you have, it should be on a dimmer – in fact it should probably be on a dimmer anyway. But you need to buy more lights: a table light for atmosphere and a floor light to throw a soft glimmer up onto your walls. You need a task light to read by and perhaps a light above a picture to show it off. Have your lights on different circuits so you can vary the mood according to what you are doing.

In short; create layers of lights that all do different jobs. Remember that a dark lampshade will throw a stronger light up and down, but if you want a softer, more ambient light you might want to consider a paler shade that will allow light to escape from all around.

Use lights as pointers to your possessions, consider what you want to illuminate and work accordingly. Light needs to come from above, below and the sides. That's all you need to remember.

5 GO TO THE DARK SIDE

Painting a small, dark room in a coat of white paint will give you a small dark room painted white. If white is to work as a brightener and lightener, it needs natural light to bounce off and create that illuminating effect. If you don't have natural light, the white can end up looking rather drab. Instead you need to find a colour.

Sometimes you just have to embrace a small dark room. Paint it dark – then it's a small, dark, dramatic room, a cosy room, a room that isn't pretending to be something it's not. You can, if you're feeling really brave, use gloss paint, which will reflect any light back rather than absorbing it back into itself.

The other thing is that dark walls will make all your artwork really pop and look amazing. And it looks great under electric light, which, if it's a small, dark room, is probably on most of the time anyway. If it's a room with a television in it, the telly will disappear on a dark wall, which is a good thing if you don't really want that to be the focal point

of the room, and it will give a slightly cinematic effect when turned on.

The point is that if it's a small, dark room you've got problems with, the chances are it's not the one you are spending the most time in, so you can afford to be bold. Dark walls work brilliantly in large rooms, too, though. My sitting room has charcoal walls and it looks great in both natural and electric light. If you follow all 10 of these tips you will totally be able to rock a dark room.

And while we're on the subject of paint, a room will look bigger if you paint it all the same colour: skirting boards, doors and picture rails.

Breaking up the walls with white trim is distracting to the eye and draws attention to the edges which, if it's a small room, will make it look smaller.

Using the same colour all over blurs the edges and makes it look larger.

6

LOOK INTO YOUR WARDROBE

One of the most common problems I come across is people not knowing what colour scheme to choose for their homes. In many ways, it's not surprising; Dulux alone has more than 3,000 shades to choose from, and when you consider all the different companies and all the variations of each shade, it's little wonder that the choice is bamboozling.

Then you get into the question of whether you want the wall to match the sofa or the rug, or the curtains or the cushions, or none of the above. But then again, that cushion is gorgeous, but there's only a tiny bit of it so wouldn't that be a bit much for the whole wall? Better to play it safe with the background colour? I know, I get it. So you start with your wardrobe.

In there you will find all the colours that you like to wear, which, in turn, means a collection of all the colours that you are comfortable with. And they don't have to be all from the same palette – clashing colours is quite the thing these days. A couple of years ago I bought a pair of silver boots. I love them and I wear them all the time. A few months ago we redecorated the bedroom. Guess what – the wallpaper is metallic silver. It looks great with the grey walls, bounces the light around and brings in a touch of the unexpected. After all, silver foil wallpaper – you don't see that everyday. And there's another thing – it's behind the bed, so I almost don't see it every day, since it's behind me for most of the time that I'm in that room. My house is a literal representation of my wardrobe. My husband? Oh, he only wears black and grey, so it works for him too.

7 HAVE FUN AND DON'T BE TOO SENSIBLE

It's vitally important to bring some fun into your home. A little bit of wit goes a long way, and I'm a firm believer in doing something out of the ordinary that is just for you. I adore the spotty stair runner I have throughout my (tall and narrow) house. It's the first thing you see when you come inside and it cheers me up every time. Stripes is nice, spots is more fun.

At the top of the stairs on the first floor is a bookshelf wallpaper by Young & Battaglia, which covers the entrance to my son's bedroom and makes it a secret door. We added skirting board to the bottom of a nondescript flat fire door and papered both the door and the wall around it to create a *trompe l'oeil* effect. It's always a great trick if someone is standing in the hall and suddenly the door opens. It's amazing how many people think it's either a bookshelf, out of the corner of their eye, or just a wall of wallpaper. First-time visitors never see it as a door.

That's the essence of what I'm talking about: do something unexpected. Have fun. Don't be afraid to do it because you're afraid you'll go off it. That way lies magnolia walls and neutral carpets, and the long, slow death of your soul.

8

A RUG FOR ALL SEASONS

Now, I'll be honest here, this is one of those tips that I preach but don't necessarily practise. I'm always intending to do it, and I know people who have, and I'm full of admiration but, here in the Mad House, we haven't quite pulled this one off yet. It's another of those brilliant Scandinavian habits that we're quite keen on in the UK, and elsewhere too come to that. Where you would have lots of warm, cosy textiles in winter – think knitted cushions, faux-fur throws, velvet and cashmere all layered onto your sofa for maximum cosiness – in summer you simply change them for lots of cotton and linen and lighter materials.

The Finns change their curtains seasonally from heavy winter drapes to lighter muslin in summer. The Danes don't go in for curtains at all, so that one doesn't apply for them. We have plain white blinds in every room, so there's nothing for me to change there. You can change rugs over, too. After all, storing a rug rolled up under a bed doesn't take up much room, and the same for cushion covers.

Christmas is the perfect time for this. You can buy really cheap and seasonal cushion covers that are perfect for a few weeks during the festivities and you can put them away again afterwards when you're over it. It's the same with Christmas lights: I have a Swedish friend who puts up masses of rope lights and star lights on 1 December, which I've always considered a little early for my taste. But she explained to me that at this time of year, when it's cold, dark and miserable, a few pretty lights dotted around instantly lifts the mood – and she's right. And it's safer than the candles that the curtain-averse Danes light all the time.

You don't have to limit yourself to Christmas, although that's probably when you can have the most fun. Think about doing it the rest of the year too: it will make you feel as though you've redecorated. If you're not going away on holiday, then you can bring the holiday feeling to your house by switching to some brightly coloured (probably cheap) cushions during the school holidays. And if you have children throwing food around at this time, you won't mind quite so much if they get damaged during playdates.

9

NO, IT SHOULDN'T MATCH

I was going to say that I'm sorry, but buying a three-piece suite is lazy and looks like you haven't thought about it. But actually I'm not remotely sorry to say that: it's true. It gives the impression that you just loaded the whole thing into the cart (virtual or otherwise) and didn't give it another thought. You don't need a three-piece suite, you need a sofa and two chairs. You can have two matching sofas and a different chair, if you like. But the point is that it should look like three individual pieces of furniture that you thought about, cared about and made a decision about.

Now, in recent years, this has become a bit of a trend when it comes to kitchen chairs, with a passion for all different types that look like they were salvaged from various skips in the neighbourhood. That was probably charming when the first few people did it, but it's become rather a cliché and now looks as though you're trying too hard to be fashionable. It also, I'm willing to bet, looks a bit like the artisan pizzeria at the end of the road.

I know, it's a minefield, this decorating lark. So here's the thing: you could have, for example, two matching Eames chairs at the ends of the table, which is reasonable because more than that would cost a fortune, and four different chairs around the sides (two might be more realistic, looking at the size of my table, but you get the drift). Or have six matching chairs in different colours. In other words, six mismatched chairs is a cliché, but one pair and four others is good.

Back in the sitting room, try to have a theme or shape or fabric to tie your furniture together. A grey sofa, a grey-and-white patterned armchair and a plain chair with wooden arms, for example. Something that basically – and this is another rule – looks like you meant it. You can have two lamps at different heights and styled with matching lampshades. All your cushions can be different. If you have a pair of chairs you can paint the legs of one of them a different colour. I have a pair of chairs in my house which I bought specifically because they came with different-coloured legs. They don't sell them any more, but you could DIY it.

By which I mean: you can be as mismatched as you like, but it has to look as though there was a decision, a thought process, a reason for what you have done. Otherwise it's just lifted from the catalogue, and if that was want you wanted to do you wouldn't be reading this book.

10

REALLY, YOUR HOME, YOUR STORY

I opened this book with a section called 'Your Home, Your Story', and this may sound completely obvious, but this really is the key to turning every house into a home. It's also the one thing that many of us don't do. We have been so conditioned (often by estate agents) into 'neutralising' our homes for sale that we often forget those personal details. Now that we are buying our homes to live in them, rather than for a quick sale, we're staying in them for longer and it's time to really think about displaying objects that we love; things that will make you feel good every time you walk through your front door.

Yes, we do have to be practical and buy sensibly for financial reasons, but don't choose a neutral carpet because you think you should. Choose it because it will really show off your furniture to its best advantage. And if it won't, buy another colour.

Fill your walls with artwork that you love, with photos of your family, your collection of Moomin mugs or the pieces of furniture you've inherited or acquired. Your home should tell your story. Let it be free to do that. When your friends walk into your house they should instantly get a sense of you and your style. If you're known for always wearing pink, use some in your home, from a bright pink wall, to painting the edges of the doors so that you only see it when they are open, there are a million ways to reflect your personality in your place. In short, design for a better version of who you actually are, not who you want to be.

I'm mad about my house. You can be mad about your house, too.

This is the most important element of all. Your home should be a reflection of who you are and who lives there. This means that you need to include pieces that you have collected through your life and have them on display as well as things that you love whether they are old or new. William Morris put it perfectly when he said, 'have nothing in your home that you do not know to be useful or believe to be beautiful.'

INDEX

PICTURE CREDITS

The publisher would like to thank the following sources for their kind permission to reproduce the photographs in this book.

Page 4 Paul Craig; 30 GAP Interiors/Costas Picadas; 36 to 37 Gap Interiors/Guillaume de Laubier; 56 GAP Interiors/House and Leisure, photographer: Elsa Young, stylist: Heather Boting; 76 to 77 GAP Interiors/Jake Fitzjones, architects: Martins Camisuli Architects and Designers, stylist: Shani Zion; 94 to 95 Haanel Cassidy/Condé Nast via Getty Images; 108 to 109 Bureaux; 117 GAP Interiors/David Cleveland; 136 to 137 GAP Interiors/Dan Duchars; 144 GAP Interiors/Jake Fitzjones; 156 to 157 Paul Craig; 175 GAP Interiors/Costas Picadas; 200 to 201 Paul Craig.

Illustration and design by Abi Read.

ACKNOWLEDGEMENTS

A huge thank you to my fabulous agent Jane Turnbull, without whom, etc. Jane and I were introduced after a long chain of emails that started with a client and finished when she agreed to help me with this – my second book, and the book of the blog.

To Stephanie Milner, Katie Cowan and Michelle Mac at Pavilion Books who embraced the challenge to 'reinvent the coffee-table interiors book'. In a sector defined by hefty tomes with glossy photographs, they were brave enough to go against the grain and publish a book that's almost all words. And just a few photos. With these very gorgeous illustrations.

Thank you, too, to Tim Webb-Jenkins, who interpreted my ideas so perfectly at a very early stage, helping me to create something that reflects the blog, my house, and me. And thank you to Abi Read, who worked with me to develop the illustrations and design. I was quite fussy. She was very patient.

Of course, no list of acknowledgements would be complete without a sincere thank you to all readers and Instagram followers of Mad About The House, many of whom have become clients, who faithfully read my ramblings at 7am, five days a week. Without you the blog wouldn't exist. And without the blog this book wouldn't exist. Thank you for reading, commenting and joining in every day. I appreciate you all more than I can say.

And what is life without friends? To Hannah, Tania and Caron, my friends in real life and Erica Davies, who I met through this strange internet world that we inhabit and whom I am honoured to also call a friend. Then there is this community of interiors bloggers, many of whom I have met in real life and who have become proper mates: Lucy Gough, who read the very first draft of the very first book and who has never ceased to be supportive and kind and wonderful ever since. Kimberly Duran, Sophie Robinson, Bianca Hall, Carole King, Arianna Trapani, Jane Rockett and Lucy St George, whose gorgeous lamp adorns both the cover of this book and my sitting room. Russell and Jordan, the 2LG who gave me my best compliment ever when they said I looked like a glamorous Bond villain and Michael Minns, of The Shoot Factory, whose great eye and gorgeous location houses give me content every week. And what would any of it be without Odysseas of Art and Hue who designed the blog and who never fails to patiently respond to my screaming emails that I have lost a picture, crashed the site or need help with an update. I am more grateful than I can say. There are more of you, there is no more space. Thank you all of you, you know who you are.

Thank you to Adam, my husband of nearly 18 years (but I put in five years of dating before that so I'm not having those written off), and my sons Isaac and Noah for always supporting and understanding and being, all three of you, the best of the best. And not forgetting Enid Cat, who has taken absolutely no notice of anything at all but who is always supremely decorative – even if she has trashed my pink velvet chaise longue.

I want to add a final word to acknowledge all those who have no homes to frame their story. Living in London, as in many other major cities, I feel an increasing sense of the gap between homeowners and homeless. Last year, I started a monthly donation to a homeless charity to try a do a tiny bit to redress the balance. Perhaps any of you who buy this book might be willing or able to give a small amount to the homeless charity of your choice in the hope that someone somewhere may also be given the chance of a home of their own.